Words FOR Women

Cover and layout design: Kristi Yoder

ISBN: 978-1-941213-75-9

Printed in the USA

Published by:
TGS International
P.O. Box 355
Berlin, Ohio 44610 USA
Phone: 330-893-4828
Fax: 330-893-2305
www.tgsinternational.com

TGS001056

WILMA WEBB

Words FOR Women

Acknowledgments

I give honor and praise to my Lord and Saviour, Jesus Christ, who put these stories and Scriptures on my heart. Many times I prayed for help, and the Lord heard. I thank all the editors for their work in perfecting this book, and TGS for believing it worthy of printing. I am indebted to my son Michael for being there to help me, and for all his encouragement. I thank my husband for reading what I wrote, and for helping me in so many ways. To God be the glory!

—*Wilma Webb*

To every woman who reads this book

I pray these devotionals will encourage you and give you a thirst for God and His living water. Only Jesus can satisfy and fulfill us. I pray you will see how important it is to allow God to shape us through life's experiences. I hope these words will encourage you on your journey, inspire you to keep the faith, and impel you to a closer walk with God.

—*a sister in Christ,*
Wilma Webb

Table of Contents

Page **Title** **Scripture** **Poem**

Part One: Intimacy with God

14	A Thirst for God	Psalm 63:1–5	Satisfied
17	Delight Thyself in the Lord	Psalm 37:1–7	How I Love Your Word
20	Blessed Is the Man	Psalm 1	Planted by the Water
23	Setting Our Love on God	Psalm 91	Walking Together
26	The Necessity of Prayer	1 Thess. 5:14–25	Holy Ground
29	Prayer and Fellowship	Psalm 34:1–10	Fellowship with God
32	The Fervent Prayer	1 Samuel 1:9–18	I Pray to My Father
35	Show Us the Father	John 14:5–11	Believe in Me
38	Christ, the Good Shepherd	John 10:1–11	The Good Shepherd
41	Christ's Body and Blood	Luke 22:15–20	Communion's Cup
44	If Ye Then Be Risen	Colossians 3:1–15	The Greatest Miracle
47	Best Friends	John 15:12–17	Come Walk with Me
50	Identification	John 15:1–8	Assurance in My Soul
53	Consider God's Wondrous Works	Job 37:1–14	Praise Him
55	Cleaning House	2 Kings 22:1–11	Pleasing Christ
58	Hidden Things	Joshua 7:1–23	Show Me
60	Famished or Filled?	John 6:26–51	The Living Bread
62	Malnourished	Psalm 119:97–104	Take Time
64	The Chocolate Bar	Matthew 7:7–11	I Come to You
67	Whose Perspective Matters?	Job 40:1–14	Keep the Faith

Part Two: Separated unto God

72	Babes in Christ	Hebrews 5:10–14	Come Closer
75	Transformed	Matthew 20:29–34	Transformed by Christ
78	A Holy People	1 Peter 1:13–21	The Lamb of God
81	A Living Sacrifice	Romans 12:1–3	Commitment
84	A Willing Heart	Exodus 35:21–29	A Willing Offering
87	A Peculiar Treasure	Titus 2:11–15	Entirely His
90	A Vacant Lot	Philippians 4:6–9	What Are We Thinking?
92	Accepting My Place	1 Cor. 11:1–15	Let Her Be Veiled

Page	Title	Scripture	Poem
95	Call to Commitment	Mark 8:34–38	His Call, Our Commitment
98	Choices	John 12:44–50	The Crossroad
101	Who Are You?	Matthew 6:1–8	We Come
104	Christmas in My Heart	Luke 2:10–20	My Christmas Joy
108	Where Hate Is Found	Genesis 37:3–11	Seeds
111	Forgiveness	Matthew 18:21–35	Relationships
114	Plucked Flowers	Galatians 5:16–25	I Go Apart
117	Clear Vision	Luke 6:36–42	Lord, Help Me See
120	Freedom	Heb. 13:7–9, 17; 1 Peter 5:5–6	Finding Freedom
122	Guilty by Association	Proverbs 1:7–19	Bear Your Cross for Jesus
124	Growing in Grace and Godliness	Ephesians 4:11–16	The Father Watches
127	Our Adornment	1 Peter 3:1–6	Jesus, I Would Learn of You
130	True Beauty	Galatians 5:22–26	True Beauty
132	Happy Are Ye	John 13:1–17	In True Humility
135	Our Tongues: Good or Evil?	James 3:1–10	The Tongue
138	Speaking Slander	Psalm 15	Keep My Tongue
141	Making a Difference	Acts 9:36–42	Love Reached Out
144	The Influence of Godly Women	2 Peter 1:3–9	What Do Folks See?
147	The Perfect Quilt	Romans 15:1–7	God's Quilt
150	Sick or Strong?	Isaiah 40:28–31	Please Do Forgive
153	Sowing and Reaping	Galatians 6:7–10	What Is Our Life?
155	Spiced Peaches	Matthew 23:23–33	The Perfect Peach
157	The Cake Disaster	James 4:5–10	Search Our Hearts
160	The Body of Christ	John 17:15–26	Jesus Prayed
163	True Worship	1 Chr. 16:23–31	Worship Christ
166	For God's Glory	Eph. 1:4–7, 12–14	Give God Glory
169	A Faithful Life	Psalm 71	Growing Older

Part Three: Loving Our Husbands

174	Love	1 John 3:16–23	Let Us Adore Him
177	Love in Action	1 John 5:1–5	Love, a Word of Action
180	"Slick" Dumplings	Ephesians 5:22–33	My Husband
183	Wise Women	Matthew 7:24–27	What Makes a Home

Page	Title	Scripture	Poem

Part Four: Loving Our Children

Page	Title	Scripture	Poem
188	The Wonder of Motherhood	Proverbs 4:7–18	Jewels Rare
191	A Gift from God	Psalm 113	Thank God
194	Communication	1 John 4:7–11, 16	Love Letters
197	Despise Not These Little Ones	Matthew 19:13–15	Faith Like a Child
200	Follow the Steps	Psalm 119:129–136	Walk in Truth
202	God Doesn't Forget	Isaiah 49:13–23	Let the Children Come to Me
205	Shutting Out the Storm	Psalm 46:1–7	A Shelter
207	Teachers of Good Things	Titus 2:1–5	Help Us
210	The Chickenpox Siege	Psalm 103	For Mothers
213	In the Night Watches	Psalm 63:1–7; 42:8	In the Night
215	Whose Servant Are You?	Matthew 25:31–46	A Servant's Heart
218	Mothers, Pray	Psalm 34:11–18	Your Mother's Prayer
221	Letting Go	1 Sam. 1:11, 20–28	Let Go

Part Five: Grace in Trials

Page	Title	Scripture	Poem
226	A Refuge	Psalm 142	Jesus
228	A Happy People	1 Peter 1:3–9	A Candle
230	And Again I Say, Rejoice	Philippians 4:1–8	There's a Song
233	Be Joyful	Isaiah 12	I Found a Treasure
236	An Odd Duck	Hebrews 11:8–16	To Live or Die
239	A Sweet Savor	Zech. 13:9; Psalm 17:3–8	Through Fire
242	Discouragement	Joshua 1:6–9	Where Is God?
245	Fear Not	Psalm 56	Fear Not, My Child
248	Comparing Ourselves	Psalm 100	Discontentment
251	Giving Thanks	Psalm 107:1–8	Without Number
254	Be Strong	Ephesians 6:10–20	O Praise His Name
257	"Lord, Save Us"	Matthew 8:23–27	The Storm
259	That Rock Was Christ	1 Cor. 10:1–13	The Rock
262	Swallowed or Surrendered?	Jonah 1:1–7	Hear and Obey
265	Do Your Best	Colossians 3:22–25	A Work for Us to Do
268	God Thinks of Me	Psalm 139:1–18	Jesus Knows Me

Page	Title	Scripture	Poem
271	When We Don't Understand	Hebrews 2:9–18	Trust
274	Contend for the Faith	Jude 3; Col. 1:10–20	Hold Fast the Faith
277	When the Dark Billows Roll	Acts 27:10–25	When the Waves Roll
280	Prisoners	Psalm 66:16–20	O Praise the Lord
282	The Lord's Battle	1 Chron. 16:8–12	Cry to God
285	An Overcomer	1 John 2:12–17	Saints, Awaken
288	God's Promises	Jeremiah 31	I Have a Friend
291	Security	Psalm 121	I Won't Worry
294	"My Peace I Leave You"	John 14:27–31	Perfect Peace

Part Six: Looking Heavenward

Page	Title	Scripture	Poem
298	The Journey of Life	Psalm 119:33–40	On a Journey
301	Learning to Drive	Proverbs 3:1–7	Keep My Focus True
304	Christ Is Risen!	Luke 24:1–11	Mary at the Tomb
307	A Heritage Forever	Colossians 1:10–14	Adopted
310	The Light	1 John 1:5–9	Jesus Is the Light
313	The Treasure Chest	1 Thess. 4:16–18	The Word of God
316	The Wild Violet	Jude 20–25	Christ's Glorious Church
319	The Completed Puzzle	Revelation 2:7–11	Persevere
321	Walk Worthy	Eph. 4:1–7, 17–24	Walk in Truth
324	Weighed in the Balances	Daniel 5	In the Balance Weighed
327	And the World Passeth Away	2 Peter 3:7–14	Found Wanting?
330	But a Step	John 5:24–29	My Soul Shall Soar
333	The Brevity of Life	Psalm 90	Teach Us to Number Our Days
336	Go Ye into All the World	Luke 15:1–10	Have I Cared Enough?
339	Anticipating	2 Peter 3:9–14	In the Twinkling of an Eye
343	Endnotes		
345	About the Author		

Part
ONE

Intimacy
with God

A Thirst
for God

I remember sweltering in the garden on a summer day. The sun blazed down, making me thirsty. I kept on working, however, doing just a bit more weeding. Finally, I could no longer ignore my craving for a drink of cold water. Throwing down my hoe, I headed to the house for a refreshing glass of water. I longed for that water more than anything else, for water satisfies the thirst like nothing else does.

Do we long after God in the same intense way? Do we thirst for His Word? The psalmist paints a vivid word picture in Psalm 42:1: "As the hart panteth after the water brooks, so panteth my soul after thee, O God." The following verse says, "My soul thirsteth for God, for the living God." Psalm 119:131 presents a similar thought: "I opened my mouth, and panted: for I longed for thy commandments."

God placed within every heart a desire, a thirst for Him; nothing but the living God will quench that thirst. In Isaiah 55:1, we hear the call of God to thirsty man: "Ho, every one that thirsteth, come ye to the waters."

Jesus, speaking to the woman of Samaria, said, "If thou knewest the gift of God, and who it is that saith to thee, Give me to drink: thou wouldest have asked of him, and he would have given thee living water" (John 4:10). Referring to the water drawn from Jacob's well, He said, "Whosoever drinketh of this water shall thirst again" (John 4:13). He said, however, "Whosoever drinketh of the water that I shall give him shall never thirst; but the water that I shall give him shall be in him a well of water springing up into everlasting life" (John 4:14).

While we live on earth, we will always need food and water. They are essential for our survival. Similarly, our spiritual life needs nourishment. We need the Bread of Heaven and the Living Water that Jesus offers. Matthew 5:6 tells us, "Blessed are they which do hunger and thirst after righteousness: for they shall be filled." Psalm 107:9 says, "For he satisfieth the longing soul, and filleth the hungry soul with goodness."

If our souls are dehydrated or malnourished, it is not God's fault, it is ours. The psalmist David expressed his desire in Psalm 40:8 when he said, "I delight to do thy will, O my God: yea, thy law is within my heart." David also said in Psalm 36:7–9, "How excellent is thy loving-kindness, O God! therefore the children of men put their trust under the shadow of thy wings. They shall be abundantly satisfied with the fatness of thy house; and thou shalt make them drink of the river of thy pleasures. For with thee is the fountain of life: in thy light shall we see light."

May we go to the Source to satisfy our thirst. We will never be disappointed.

Satisfied

How precious are the times we meet
To sit and learn at Jesus' feet,

To hear Him speak with words of love,
And feel His peace sent from above.

Within His warmth and love I bask.
What more could I, His daughter, ask?

To know He dwells within my breast
Brings perfect peace and joy and rest.

O what a joy supreme, sublime
To fellowship with Christ divine!

For nothing else can satisfy
My thirsting soul, my inner cry.

O come to Christ, and you will find
He'll give you joy and peace of mind;

Abundant life He offers you;
O come and see—you'll find it's true.

Delight Thyself
in the Lord

salm 37 provides a formula for our walk with God that, if followed, will enhance our relationship with Him and keep us thirsting for Him. Verse 3 tells us to trust in the Lord. Do we believe with all our hearts that He is the Almighty God? Is anyone greater or stronger than He? Of course not! So we must not fret, but trust, and we will be fed and cared for in every way.

In verse 4 we read, "Delight thyself also in the LORD; and he shall give thee the desires of thine heart." How do we delight ourselves in the Lord? As I thought about this, I remembered my babies. I was blessed with seven of them. I remember holding them as infants, gazing at them, noticing their every feature. How I rejoiced when they gave me their first smiles, sat up alone, or took that first step on their own. I delighted in them. My life seemed to revolve around those precious babies. I dropped whatever I was doing to change their diapers or to feed them. Isn't it a mother's joy to do this?

Now, how do we delight in our Lord? Does our whole life revolve around Him? Is it a delight to do His will, or would we rather do something that pleases ourselves? Do we make our plans for the day without first consulting God? Maybe He has something else in mind for the day.

Considering how we revel in all that a baby does and is, we must ask ourselves if we rejoice in who God is and what He does in our lives. Do we search His Word for hidden riches? Do we seek His face, His character, His purpose, and His plan for us? Or do we just skim the surface, hardly finding enough food and water to keep us alive?

The next command is found in verse 5—we are to commit our way unto the Lord. We have to relinquish our own will. This isn't always easy. Too often we want to be in control. Instead of taking charge of our lives, we are to roll every care and burden upon the Lord. He is far more capable than we are of orchestrating our affairs.

Verse 7 says, "Rest in the LORD, and wait patiently for Him." We are to be still and wait for Him to work. We are not to worry or fret, wishing we could take things into our own hands. Just relax, and trust the One to whom we have committed all.

No matter where we find ourselves in life, no matter what the trials we face, we need to keep our hunger and thirst for God. He is the only One who can satisfy our souls. Like David, we should thirst for God as intensely as a deer who pants for the water brooks (Psalm 42:1–2).

May we always follow the formula: trust in the Lord, delight ourselves in Him, commit our way unto Him, and rest in Him. Then we will be able to say as David did in Psalm 40:8, "I delight to do thy will, O my God: yea, thy law is within my heart." Psalm 119:103 expresses David's delight in God's Word, "How sweet are thy words unto my taste! yea, sweeter than honey to my mouth!" Psalm 34:8 says, "O taste and see that the LORD is good: blessed is the man that trusteth in him."

How I Love Your Word

O how I love your Word, O Lord;
It is my chief delight
To learn your truths so I can walk
Your path that's filled with light.

O how I love your Word, O Lord,
To read how Jesus came
To heal the sick and sinful ones,
The deaf, the blind, the lame.

But most of all, I love to read
How Jesus bought my soul,
When, bowed beneath His Father's will,
He bled to make me whole.

My heart is full of praise when I
Read how my Lord arose.
He broke the chains of sin and death,
And conquered all my foes.

O how I love your Word, O Lord,
It is a treasure rare;
I'll feast upon it every day,
And of its wealth I'll share.

Blessed
Is the Man

When we moved to our current residence a few years ago, the only trees that shaded our yard were three scraggly pines. Since my husband enjoys planting trees and watching them grow, several trees now grace our property. Our home sits on a slight incline, so my husband had to be diligent to water each tree after planting it. Even so, we lost a few trees during a prolonged drought one summer. We watched the maple tree's leaves shrivel up and die, and the pine tree's needles grow brown and brittle.

Psalm 1:1–3 says, "Blessed is the man that walketh not in the counsel of the ungodly, nor standeth in the way of sinners, nor sitteth in the seat of the scornful. But his delight is in the law of the LORD; and in his law doth he meditate day and night. And he shall be like a tree planted by the rivers of water, that bringeth forth his fruit in his season; his leaf also shall not wither; and whatsoever he doeth shall prosper." Jeremiah 17:7–8 echoes this theme: "Blessed is the man that trusteth in the LORD, and whose hope the LORD is. For he shall be as a tree planted by the waters, and that spreadeth out her roots by the river, and shall not see when heat cometh, but her leaf shall be green; and shall not be careful in the year of drought, neither shall cease from yielding fruit."

Each of these men is compared to a tree planted by a water source. There, the tree can extend his roots to the water. When drought comes, the tree is not affected by the lack of rain, for his roots draw up life-sustaining water. His leaves will not wither, but will even remain green during drought. While lack of rain causes other trees to be barren, the tree by the river will yield his fruit as usual.

God cares for those who honor Him and His Word, who choose to follow Him and trust in Him. God never neglects His children. He provides all they need to live and grow and produce fruit.

The Bible also speaks of the transgressor, or sinner. Isaiah 1:28 tells us that he will be consumed. Verse 30 compares the transgressor to an oak tree whose leaf fades, and to a garden that has no water. Jesus said that the fig tree that did not bear fruit would be cut down (Luke 13:7–9). Another time He spoke of Himself as the Vine and of His followers as the branches. The branches that did not abide in Him were cast out and burned (John 15:6).

Why would we not choose to follow the Lord? Isaiah 58:11 promises blessing to those who do right: "And the LORD shall guide thee continually, and satisfy thy soul in drought, and make fat thy bones: and thou shalt be like a watered garden, and like a spring of water, whose waters fail not."

Jesus offers us living water to sustain our souls. In Christ, there is no lack. We can sink our roots down deep into His water. Even in the midst of difficult, trying times, we won't become barren, shriveled-up people. We will bring forth fruit to glorify God.

Blessed is the woman who puts her trust in God and chooses to walk in His way. She will never regret it.

Planted by the Water

The tree grew tall and stately
Along the riverside;
She spread her branches over
The rolling countryside.

When drought consumed the landscape,
And trees around grew bare,
The tree beside the river
Stood like a lady fair.

Her leaves refused to wither,
For deep beneath the ground
Her roots absorbed the moisture,
Where hidden streams abound.

If we will seek the water
That Jesus' love provides,
And feed upon His wisdom,
We will be well supplied.

No matter what the weather,
If rain or drought appear,
The Lord will make us prosper,
Throughout the driest year.

Setting Our
Love on God

*P*salm 91:14 says, "Because he hath set his love upon me, therefore will I deliver him: I will set him on high, because he hath known my name." When I read the first phrase of this verse, I asked myself, *Am I doing this?* How do I set my love upon God? Isn't it by putting Him first in my life? I thought of how I begin the day. Is my first thought, *God, thank you for this day?* Too often my thoughts are busy with what I need to do that day, or even tomorrow's demands. What an ungrateful person I am! God deserves our first thoughts.

Thinking about God, however, or praising Him for all He's done for us, is not enough. Our actions are the real proof that we have set our love upon God. Are we obeying His Word? Do our lives and actions show that we follow His teachings and commandments? God wants our hearts to focus on loving and pleasing Him.

Do we know God's name? This means to know God intimately. We can talk of God and yet not understand all it means to know His name. Of course, we can never fully know or understand God, but we should seek to know Him better and more intimately every day.

What a thought—to know God! If we have come to Christ and have a relationship with God, then we have started on the journey of knowing Him. We all have acquaintances with whom we may exchange greetings, chat briefly, or share some surface concerns. Jesus wants to be more than that to us. He wants to be our best friend.

When we dig deep into God's Word, we learn to know Him better. How wonderful that when we do this, we find our love for Him growing stronger. We find our thoughts dwelling on Him throughout the day and even at night when we awake. Our earnest desire will be to please Him—to set our love upon Him.

This does not please Satan, so he will try to divert our attention onto other things, including legitimate things. Beware! The Bible says in 1 Peter 5:8, "Be vigilant; because your adversary the devil, as a roaring lion, walketh about, seeking whom he may devour." Satan wants not only to pull us away from God, but he also wants to devour us. But God is greater; in Him we can stand and overcome.

God promises, "Therefore will I deliver him: I will set him on high" (Psalm 91:14). When I read this verse, I pictured a small child in deep water, whose father reaches down and sets him on a high rock. When we are in trouble, this is what God does for us. He delivers us, placing us on the Rock, Christ Jesus.

Psalm 91:15 tells us that God is also with us *in* our troubles. He gives us grace, and sustaining power to be faithful and true. He will deliver us in His time. May we set our love upon God. He will never fail to care for His own.

Walking Together

I walk with Jesus on life's way;
He grows more precious every day.
I tell Him all my grief and woe,
He whispers that He loves me so.

Each day I journey by His side,
Content with Jesus I'll abide.
While basking in His love so dear,
I thank Him that He drew me near.

He knows just what I need each day
For trials that will come my way.
Alone I cannot face my foes,
And so with me, my Saviour goes.

It's such a joy to walk this road,
To share with Him my heavy load.
What fellowship and peace I've found,
I feel like I'm on holy ground.

So come, my friend, and know Him too;
I know He wants to walk with you.
He longs to hold you always near,
To fill your life with hope and cheer.

The Necessity
of Prayer

In Psalm 73:28, the psalmist testifies, "But it is good for me to draw near to God." Prayer is one way we draw closer to God. As we go throughout the day, prayer should rise from our hearts. We might not be kneeling—especially if we're cooking a meal, washing dishes, or folding laundry. Others may not hear us speak a word, but in our hearts we are communing with God.

Prayer is essential to our spiritual health and for the strengthening of other Christians. 1 Thessalonians 5:17 reminds us, "Pray without ceasing." Prayer should become such a habit for us that it is easy to talk to God, sharing everything with Him.

Sometimes our prayers are for ourselves. Jonah prayed for himself as he lay wrapped in seaweed in the fish's belly. He prayed, believing God would hear him and deliver him (Jonah 2:1).

At other times, our prayers are for others. Job prayed for his two friends who had misjudged him when they declared he was suffering the consequences of his sin. God told them to ask Job to pray for them. Job held no hard feelings toward his friends for their accusations, for he willingly prayed for them. Then God blessed Job, giving him twice as much as he had before (Job 42:10).

At times we need to ask for the prayers of others. When Daniel was commanded to reveal to the king his dream, Daniel asked his two friends to pray, ". . . to desire the mercies of the God of heaven" (Daniel 2:18). Daniel prayed again, thanking God, when God revealed to him the king's dream (Daniel 2:20–23).

Paul requested the Colossians to continue in prayer for him that God would give him opportunities to speak of Christ (Colossians 4:3). Though Paul was in bonds, God answered this prayer by allowing Paul to speak of Christ, even to kings.

We need specific times that we concentrate on reading God's Word and praying. Psalm 55:17 tells us that David prayed in the evening, in the morning, and at noon. Daniel, too, was accustomed to praying three times a day. Even after the king made a decree that for thirty days no one could pray to or make a petition of anyone except the king, Daniel continued his practice of prayer. With his windows open, Daniel prayed to God. Obeying God was more important than placating the king.

Years ago, I read the true story of a woman who was awakened from sleep with the urge to pray for someone in great danger. Although she did not know who it was, she prayed earnestly. She wrote the date and time in her journal, wondering if she would ever know for whom she had prayed. Sometime later, she heard a missionary tell how he had faced danger in which death had seemed imminent. Suddenly, the danger was gone. Those who had threatened him said later that his jeep had been surrounded by shining white beings with swords. They were afraid to go near him. This took place at the very moment when the woman was praying for someone in danger.

Yes, prayer is needed for ourselves and others. Prayer is one of our greatest weapons to defeat the enemy. It is an avenue to a closer walk with God. We cannot survive spiritually without our lifeline to God. May we use it often.

Holy Ground

Walking down the road of life,
Seeing all the sin and strife,
I am glad that I have found
A place where there is holy ground.

When the stress of life crowds in,
I'm surrounded by man's sin,
There's a place where I can flee,
Finding rest on bended knee.

Every time I am distressed,
And I long for quiet rest,
I can bow my head and pray,
Know that help is on the way.

Jesus hears me when I cry,
Understands when I ask, "Why?"
Then He calms my every fear,
Saying, "Child, to me draw near."

O that place of hallowed ground
Where God's mercy can be found;
O the joy that I can know
When I to the Saviour go.

When He's soothed my troubled cries,
I often hesitate to rise
And leave that place of hallowed prayer,
For with me God has tarried there.

Prayer and *Fellowship*

What role does prayer play in your life? Prayer is talking to God. It is also a way to worship Him. One result of prayer is fellowship with God. The word *fellowship* means "companionship, sharing, familiarity, intimacy, comradeship, friendship, or brotherhood."[1]

I knew an older lady whose radiant spirit drew me like a magnet. Time spent in her presence was as refreshing as a drink of cold water. She loved to talk about how precious Jesus was to her, and what she was learning from His Word.

David must have had this kind of intimacy with God. In Psalm 143:8, David prayed, "Cause me to hear thy lovingkindness in the morning; for in thee do I trust: cause me to know the way wherein I should walk; for I lift up my soul unto thee." David began his day with prayer, seeking God's direction for his life. He prayed, "Teach me to do thy will; for thou art my God" (Psalm 143:10).

Throughout the Psalms, we see David coming to God in all kinds of situations. Sometimes he was pursued by his enemies, and he prayed for deliverance. At other times he was discouraged, or his heart was overflowing with praise to God. We read his prayers of repentance and his desire that God would restore his spirit. David often expressed his trust in God. He continually communed with God, finding in God's presence a closeness, a warmth, and a friendship that he could find nowhere else.

Psalm 63:1–8 describes David's relationship with God. He said of God, "Early will I seek thee: my soul thirsteth for thee, my flesh longeth for thee in a dry and thirsty land, where no water is; . . . thy lovingkindness is better than life, my lips shall praise thee. Thus will I bless thee while I live: I will lift up my hands in thy name. My soul shall be satisfied . . ." (Psalm 63:1, 3–5).

Prayer is not a one-way street. When we pray asking God for something, we want to receive an answer to that prayer. What do we give to God when we pray? Do we open our hearts to Him, sharing everything with Him? Do we worship God? Do we express our love to Him, thanking Him for who He is and all He does for us? Do we praise Him, giving Him all our devotion? The more we commune with God, the better we come to know Him, and the closer our fellowship with Him. The more we read and study God's Word, the easier we find it to pray and to understand what He says to us.

Psalm 95:6–7 invites, "O come, let us worship and bow down: let us kneel before the LORD our maker. For he is our God; and we are the people of his pasture, and the sheep of his hand." Isaiah 43:1, 7 tells us, "Fear not: for I have redeemed thee, I have called thee by thy name; thou art mine. Even every one that is called by my name: for I have created him for my glory, I have formed him; yea, I have made him." Jesus says in John 16:27 that the Father loves us because we have loved Christ and believe that He came from God. God desires our fellowship, for He created us. May we find our relationship with Him growing deeper and richer as we spend time in prayer.

Fellowship with God

The fellowship that we can know,
As in His Word we daily grow,
Is far beyond my tongue to tell,
But in my heart deep praises swell.

To think that God should even care
To hear my humble, childish prayer;
To know He holds me in His hand,
Is more than I can understand.

But, oh, the joy transcending all
To know Christ hears my faintest call!
He sees my deepest, hidden fear,
And softly whispers, "I am here."

The Fervent
Prayer

How often do we pray without actually expecting an answer? Prayer can become a mere recitation of words or a list of people or situations that we mention to God. James 5:16 tells us, "The effectual fervent prayer of a righteous man availeth much." God knows our hearts. He knows whether or not our prayers are earnest. To pray *fervently* means to pray "passionately, ardently, eagerly, and enthusiastically."[2]

In today's reading, Hannah said, "I . . . have poured out my soul before the LORD" (1 Samuel 1:15). Her words were not even audible, but God heard her fervent prayer and answered the cry of her heart. Later, Hannah said of her son Samuel, "For this child I prayed" (1 Samuel 1:27).

Acts 12 tells how Peter had been thrown into prison where he was guarded by two soldiers. The church had heard of Peter's imprisonment and had gathered for a prayer meeting. Their prayers rose unceasingly to God. They earnestly prayed for their brother Peter. As Peter lay chained between two soldiers, the angel of the Lord came, smote him on his side, and said, "Arise up quickly." Peter's chains fell from his hands. The angel led Peter through the first and second wards out to the iron gate that led into the city. The gate swung open, and Peter and the angel passed through. What a miraculous deliverance! Was it because the church was praying?

Our Saviour prayed what was perhaps His most earnest prayer as He knelt in the garden of Gethsemane. Christ knew He would need to drink a bitter cup, the cup of an agonizing death for our sins. He struggled as He prayed, and His sweat was as it were great drops of blood falling to the ground. But He won the battle by yielding to His Father, saying, "Not my will, but thine, be done" (Luke 22:42).

Prayer is essential to our spiritual wellbeing. Before Jesus entered the garden to pray, He told the disciples, "Watch and pray, that ye enter not into temptation" (Matthew 26:41). He knew they would try, but fail, for Jesus said, "The spirit indeed is willing, but the flesh is weak" (Matthew 26:41). When Christ was arrested, all His disciples fled.

Prayer is part of the armor of God that we are to put on so we can withstand temptation and evil. As we pray for ourselves and for the saints, we are endued with fortitude. God gives us courage and boldness to stand for Him and to be His witnesses.

Sometimes our hearts are so burdened that we don't even know how to pray, how to express the turmoil within us. What comfort to know that the Holy Spirit intercedes for us according to the will of God (Romans 8:26–27).

May we not take lightly the command to pray. 1 Timothy 2:8 says, "I will therefore that men pray every where, lifting up holy hands, without wrath and doubting." God wants us to pray for all men, but when we do so, our hands must be clean and free from sin. We must not harbor resentment or doubt. *Doubt* here means "disputing." If we are not at peace with others, we need to confess and be reconciled before we can pray for others.

Finally, my dear sisters, let's be strong in the Lord. Through prayer we can find His strength to keep us faithful unto the end.

I Pray to My Father

I pray to my Father at morning's light,
When I feel like singing and all is bright.
Sweet praises I offer from heart that's full,
For life is a blessing, and all is right.

I pray to my Father when skies are gray,
When I'm needing a friend to hold my hand.
He gives me assurance and draws me close;
I know that He loves me, and understands.

I pray to my Father when storm clouds come,
When I need a shelter, He's by my side;
I know He will keep me when all looks dim,
For Christ is my Refuge, in Him I'll hide.

I pray to my Father when raindrops fall,
When I'm crushed by sorrow, and joy has fled.
Though I cry in anguish, I know He cares;
His Son came for us, His blood to shed.

I pray to my Father when fog is dense,
I can't see the way, I don't know His plan.
Still then I will trust, and believe He knows best;
In faith I'll keep clinging to His strong hand.

I'll pray to my Father at eventide,
When death hovers near me, I will not fear.
For God is my Father, He calls me His own;
I'll rest in His promise that He is here.

Show Us
the Father

*J*esus had been telling His disciples that He would soon leave them to go to His Father. Some of them still did not understand that Jesus was the way to the Father. Jesus said, "I am the way, the truth, and the life: no man cometh unto the Father, but by me. If ye had known me, ye should have known my Father also: and from henceforth ye know him, and have seen him." Philip persisted, saying, "Lord, shew us the Father" (John 14:6–8).

Jesus explained to them that if they had seen Him, they had seen the Father. As we read the Bible, we glimpse a picture of Jesus—not His facial features or hair color, but a portrayal of His character which reveals much about the Father.

In Matthew 9:35–36, we read how Jesus went into cities and villages teaching and preaching the Gospel of the kingdom. He healed sickness and disease among the people. When He saw the throngs of people, Jesus was moved with compassion, not only because of their physical needs, but also because of their need of a Saviour. Our God is a God of compassion.

Matthew 19:13–15 shows us Jesus' love for little children. He spent time with them, taking them in His arms and blessing them. Our God is a kind and loving God.

When Jesus cast out the moneychangers and vendors who were desecrating the temple, He showed us that He is righteous and holy (Luke 19:45–46). Likewise, Christ wants our temple—our heart and body—to be set apart for Him so He can abide there and be honored.

We see Jesus' patience as He taught the disciples again and again when they seemed slow to grasp His words. Jesus exercised discipline, often retreating alone to pray to His Father. He fasted for forty days, preparing for His ministry (Luke 4:2). Jesus was always doing His Father's business. He was patient, longsuffering, and forgiving with the multitudes. When Jesus healed people, He often said, "Thy sins be forgiven thee." (See Matthew 9:2; Mark 2:5.) He taught that we, too, must forgive others as often as they offend us. Our God is gracious to forgive us when we come to Him.

Throughout the Old and New Testaments, we find words that describe Jesus and the Father. He is called Emmanuel, King of kings, Deliverer, Prince of Peace, Everlasting Father, Lamb of God, Alpha and Omega, and many other titles.

How precious the promise Christ gives in John 14:23, "If a man love me, he will keep my words: and my Father will love him, and we will come unto him, and make our abode with him." To know Jesus is to know the Father. We know the Father loves us, for He sent His only begotten Son to die for us. By believing on Christ, we can live and partake of His marvelous mercy and grace, and inherit eternal life. 2 Corinthians 4:6 says, "For God, who commanded the light to shine out of darkness, hath shined in our hearts, to give the light of the knowledge of the glory of God in the face of Jesus Christ." If we know Jesus, we know and have seen the Father.

Believe in Me
(from John 14–15)

Christ Jesus said, "I'm going
To my Father's home on high,
To prepare unnumbered mansions;
You can come there by and by."

They said, "Lord, where's the Father,
And please, tell us the way,
We don't know where you're going,
How can we know the way?"

Then Christ in love rebuked them:
"I'm the Truth, the Life, the Way,
And if you'd see the Father,
Believe in me today.

"For, lo, I'm in the Father,
And the Father is in me;
Believe, and you'll inhabit
My home eternally.

"Soon I'll go to my Father,
For you then I will pray;
He'll send to you His Spirit
To live with you always."

Christys,
the Good Shepherd

*L*ike today's reading, Psalm 23 also speaks of the Lord as our Shepherd. In both passages we see how He cares for the sheep, providing green pastures and refreshing waters. Even when danger threatens or death is near, the Shepherd is there to protect us. God's goodness overflows; His sheep are assured of a place with Him forever.

A good shepherd does whatever is necessary to provide for his sheep. While David was shepherding his father's sheep, first a bear, and later a lion, stole a lamb from the flock. David went after them and delivered the lamb, killing the bear and the lion (1 Samuel 17:34–35). David, a good shepherd, was willing to put his life in danger to rescue a lamb.

Isaiah 53:6 speaks of us being like sheep, choosing our own way, living in sin and for self. However, Christ, the Good Shepherd, stepped in to deliver us. He was willing to take upon Himself our sin and guilt, laying down His life for us. He paid the ultimate price to redeem us.

Jesus said, "I am the good shepherd: the good shepherd giveth his life for the sheep" (John 10:11). Jesus gave his life willingly for the sheep. He says in verse 18, "No man taketh it from me, but I lay it down of myself. I have power to lay it down, and I have power to take it again."

Jesus also called Himself the Door of the sheepfold. In John 10:9, He says, "I am the door: by me if any man enter in, he shall be saved, and shall go in and out, and find pasture." Christ is the only way to salvation. Others who claim to be the way are like the thief Jesus mentions in John 10:10, who comes ". . . to steal, and to kill, and to destroy." Jesus said that He came ". . . that they might have life, and that they might have it more abundantly" (John 10:10).

Jesus came first to the Jewish people, but He also came for the whole world. Christ said of all who hear His voice and come, "There shall be one fold, and one shepherd" (John 10:16). How wonderful that Jesus loves each one of us and wants to be our Good Shepherd. We do not have to be that sheep gone astray, but we can belong to the Good Shepherd who cares and provides for His own. We are not able to take care of ourselves. We need the Shepherd's protection and, most of all, His blood to cleanse us and make us His own.

With Paul in Hebrews 13:20–21, I offer this prayer, "Now the God of peace, that brought again from the dead our Lord Jesus, that great shepherd of the sheep, through the blood of the everlasting covenant, make you perfect in every good work to do his will, working in you that which is wellpleasing in his sight, through Jesus Christ; to whom be glory for ever and ever. Amen."

The Good Shepherd

Beside the still waters, or in pastures green,
The Shepherd is leading wherever He deems.
I trust in His wisdom, He knows what is best;
He knows when I'm weary, and gives me sweet rest.

He is my Good Shepherd; He loves me, I know.
He cares for my needs and protects me from foes.
His presence, it comforts and settles my fear;
Contented, I rest when the Shepherd is near.

The Shepherd entreats me in words clear and strong
To draw me back to Him when I would do wrong.
Beside Him I'm safe; I am happy to stay;
I'll heed the Good Shepherd and gladly obey.

He's still seeking lambs that have wandered astray;
He longs for them all to return home today.
Although they have wandered away in the cold,
The Shepherd invites them, "Come back to the fold."

He'll bind up their wounds and He'll lead them once more;
Beside the still waters, they'll rest evermore.
There's no better place for the hungry to feed
Than with the Good Shepherd who meets every need.

If that lost lamb is you, oh, won't you come back,
Before wolves and ravenous lions attack?
The Good Shepherd loves you—your needs He'll supply
Return to His arms and you won't have to die.

Christ's
Body and Blood

It was communion Sunday. I listened as the minister read the prophecy in Isaiah 53:5–6, "But he was wounded for our transgressions, he was bruised for our iniquities: the chastisement of our peace was upon him; and with his stripes we are healed. All we like sheep have gone astray; we have turned everyone to his own way; and the LORD hath laid on him the iniquity of us all." The minister read a few more verses, but in my mind the words resounded, "The iniquity of us all." My sins and yours, and the sins of the entire world, were laid on Jesus.

Then I heard the words of Jesus when He said, "Take, eat: this is my body, which is broken for you" (1 Corinthians 11:24). *Broken.* I pondered that. *Broken for me. They beat you, Lord. Your back was laid open for me. They mocked you, spit in your face, put a crown of thorns on your head. I am unworthy, Lord, that you suffered thus for me.* Then we were standing and the minister was praying, blessing the communion bread. As I received my piece of bread, in my mind I saw Christ's body, broken for me—but not for me alone, but for all who would believe, all those who would become His church.

Now the minister was holding up the cup, speaking the words Jesus had said to His disciples that night long ago: "This cup is the new testament in my blood: this do ye, as oft as ye drink it, in remembrance of me" (1 Corinthians 11:25). Christ's blood—blood that was shed on Calvary as they nailed Him to the cross and pierced His side with a sword—became the cleansing fountain for the sins of mankind.

Jesus prayed for His disciples and for all those who would believe in Him. He prayed we would be one with each other and with Him, even as He and the Father are one (John 17:21). For this, Christ shed His blood, allowed His body to be broken—to reconcile us to the Father. Jesus' love and obedience surpass all others'. His sacrifice was all for us, because He and the Father loved us.

Unworthiness flooded over me. Then gratefulness and joy sprang up within me, and praises filled my being. 1 Corinthians 10:16–17 says, "The cup of blessing which we bless, is it not the communion of the blood of Christ? The bread which we break, is it not the communion of the body of Christ? For we being many are one bread, and one body: for we are all partakers of that one bread."

As we become one with Christ and the Father and with each other, we are a joy to Christ. It was for this that He laid down His life. We can never repay Him for His great gift to us. Obedience and faithfulness to His Word should flow out of our thankful hearts. Then Communion truly becomes precious to us—precious because of Christ's sacrifice, because of His love, and because we are a part of the body of Christ, purchased with His blood. Let's remember this and rejoice in the life we have in Christ Jesus.

Communion's Cup

I'm too unworthy to approach
The Lord's communion cup;
It's only by the blood of Christ
That I can dare to sup.

His blood alone avails for me
To take my sins away.
I have no merit of my own;
My debt I could not pay.

I thank the Lord for loving me
So much He came to die,
For being that pure, spotless Lamb
That perfect sacrifice.

So when I drink communion's cup,
And when I eat its bread,
I'll think about the blood Christ shed,
And thorns upon His head.

I'll not forget the stripes He bore
Upon His back for me,
So I could know salvation's grace,
And live eternally.

If Ye Then
Be Risen

How wonderful to come to Christ, finding new life in Him. This is the very essence of Christianity. Without Christ there is no true happiness or hope of life eternal. Colossians 3:1 tells us, "If ye then be risen with Christ, seek those things which are above, where Christ sitteth on the right hand of God."

Consider our unsaved state. We were entangled in the things of this world like an animal caught in a trap. There was no way to free ourselves; we needed someone to rescue us. That is what Christ did for us when we cried out to Him. Now we are lifted from the pit of sin and death to new life in Christ. What now? Do we continue in our old life and desires? No! Paul admonishes us in this passage to set our affection on things above.

Becoming a Christian is only the first step in our walk with God. Satan wants to draw us back into his trap, so we must make an effort to keep our thoughts and desires centered on Christ and heaven. We are to put off, or discontinue, walking the way we did before we came to Christ (Colossians 3:5–6). We know where that path led us—right into Satan's trap. Instead, we are to live a life patterned after Christ. As we yield ourselves to Christ, laying down the will of the flesh, Christ clothes us with His righteousness. We will put on mercy, kindness, humbleness, meekness, longsuffering, forbearance, forgiveness, charity (love), and thankfulness. (See Colossians 3:12–15.) Peace will rule in our hearts. What a different life we will live when we are risen in Christ and He reigns in our hearts.

We must feast on God's Word and cry out to Him daily for grace to stand for Him. We must never forget the goal that is set before us. May we keep our eyes on Jesus and our feet on the path to heaven. If we seek to please and honor Christ in all we do, we will someday know the joy of finishing this race and receiving the crown of everlasting life.

If ye then be risen, seek those things above,
Leaving far behind you all the stain of sin.
Keep your eyes on Jesus, walking in His love;
Find in Him endurance, the race of life to win.

The Greatest Miracle

The greatest miracle I've known
Was when I grasped the truth that I
Could be a child of the Most High.
Christ took on Him the sins I owned;
His blood for me became the flow
That washed my heart like spotless snow.

I can't forget the peace that came
The day I cried—repentance true—
When Christ absolved me through and through.
Amid the tears of guilt and shame,
The loving Saviour heard my cry,
Forgiving all. That's why He died.

My life has changed; yes, all is new—
Now all I think, and do, and say
Is done for Christ, and done His way.
Sometimes I fail; I know it's true,
But I've found mercy at His feet,
And blest communion, oh, so sweet.

Best Friends

I grew up in a small town. Each day after school, my best friend and I would walk home together. We didn't live far apart, so one day I would walk half of the way toward her house, and the next day she would walk with me part way. It was hard to part, for we had so much to share. In the evening when we were not together, my best friend and I even wrote notes to give each other the following day. If my family had had a phone, I suppose we would have called each other too.

A best friend is one with whom you share your heart. The Bible tells us that God has this kind of friend too. When mankind had become so wicked that God regretted making them, His heart was grieved. Genesis 6:8 tells us that Noah found grace in the eyes of the Lord. Verse 9 says, "Noah was a just man and perfect in his generations, and Noah walked with God." Perhaps Noah and God were walking together when God told Noah that He was going to destroy the earth with a great flood. God also told Noah what to do so that he and his family would be preserved.

James 2:23 records another friend: "Abraham believed God, and it was imputed unto him for righteousness: and he was called the Friend of God." Abraham was ninety-nine years old when God told him, "Walk before me, and be thou perfect" (Genesis 17:1). Abraham fell on his face, and God talked with him (Genesis 17:1–14). God promised to make Abraham the father of a great nation.

Genesis 5:21–24 tells of Enoch, the father of Methuselah. Verse 24 says, "And Enoch walked with God: and he was not; for God took him." Enoch was known for his life of communion with God. Evidently he did not die a normal death, but God took him to heaven.

Elijah, God's prophet, did not die either. God told him to be ready, for He was going to send down a fiery chariot and horses and take Elijah home to heaven (2 Kings 2:1). God was a faithful friend to Elijah. Earlier in Elijah's life when he had to flee Queen Jezebel's wrath, God had sent an angel to feed him. That food had sustained him on the journey of forty days and forty nights until he reached the place to which God had sent him. There by the brook Cherith, God had commanded ravens to bring him bread and meat morning and evening (1 Kings 17:1-6). God had listened to Elijah as friends do, even when Elijah complained that he was all alone, believing all the other prophets had been slain. Then God had encouraged him, telling him He had seven thousand in Israel who had not bowed the knee to Baal (1 Kings 19:12, 18). In return, Elijah was a faithful friend to God, obeying His voice, and standing for Him even in difficult times.

Moses also had a close relationship with God. After Moses had been in God's presence, his face shone so brightly that people could not bear to look at him (Exodus 34:29-35). One time God placed Moses in a cleft of a rock, putting His hand over Moses until He passed by so that Moses could see God's back (Exodus 33:22–23). God told Moses that he was going to die before the children of Israel entered Canaan. Deuteronomy 34:6 records how God buried Moses and no one ever found his burial place.

In John 15, Jesus calls us His friends. In verse 15, Jesus says, "But I have called you friends; for all things that I have heard of my Father I have made known unto you." Isn't that what friends do? They share the thoughts of their hearts. Christ showed us His love by laying down His life for us. If we keep Christ's commandments, we are His friends (verse 14).

Earthly friends will fail us. David experienced this: "Yea, mine own familiar friend, in whom I trusted, which did eat of my bread, hath lifted up his heel against me" (Psalm 41:9). Proverbs 18:24, however, tells us, "There is a friend that sticketh closer than a brother." How wonderful that we can be friends of God through Jesus Christ His Son.

Come Walk with Me

Come walk with me through meadows green
And see the flowers blooming there.
Behold the beauty of each one;
A king's attire is not as fair.

Come walk with me beside the stream
And taste its water cold and clear.
You'll find it satisfies your thirst.
The water's sweet, my child; draw near.

Come walk with me through desert bare
Where scorching heat and wind assail.
I'll not forsake you, precious child;
You'll find my grace will never fail.

Come walk with me by weary ways,
And through life's valleys dark and deep;
Fear not the path that you must take,
I made the hills; they're not too steep.

When comes the last day of your life,
I'll say, "My child, come walk with me;
On golden streets, we two shall stroll,
Together through eternity."

Identification

When we meet a person for the first time, we are curious about who they are, where they are from, what they do, and whether we have any mutual acquaintances. Sometimes we identify someone by his profession, saying, "That's my teacher, or there's the plumber." When we think of Eve, the mother of all living, we quickly label her as "the one who ate the forbidden fruit." Whatever else she did, that act became her identifying trademark. Our actions may identify us to other people, but God uses a different identification system.

I think of Mary, the mother of Jesus. One day when Jesus and His mother were at a wedding at Cana, the host ran out of wine. Mary informed Jesus of the dilemma, hoping He would produce more wine so the host would not be embarrassed. Out of respect to His mother and because of the need, Jesus turned water into wine. This was Christ's first miracle. Later, however, Mary and some of Jesus' brothers and sisters came to the house where Jesus was teaching and called for Him to come out to them. Jesus replied, "Who is my mother, or my brethren? For whosoever shall do the will of God, the same is my brother, and my sister, and mother" (Mark 3:33, 35).

Mary could not depend on her identity as Jesus' mother to gain favor with God. Who we are related to, or who we know will not matter on the Day of Judgment. We will not be able to stand on our own laurels, our good deeds, or our status as a church member or Sunday school teacher. Sometimes people may receive special treatment or discounts because of their relationship with someone. With God there is no partiality. We all have to meet the same requirements. Jesus' earthly family also needed to believe that He was the Christ. Only then would they become a part of God's family.

I remember when my husband used to have church services at our county jail. He had to be approved, and then he received a nametag with his picture. If he wanted access to the cells, he had to wear that nametag. That was his identification. We need to be identified with Christ if we want access to heaven. Jesus says in John 14:23, "If a man love me, he will keep my words: and my Father will love him, and we will come unto him, and make our abode with him." In John 15, Jesus compares Himself to a vine and His followers to branches. If the branch does not stay attached to the vine, it cannot bear fruit. So we must abide in Christ, and He will abide in us. Only then can we be fruitful Christians. This is our identification—Christ in us. John 3:16 says that whosoever believes in Christ shall not perish, but have everlasting life. John 14:21 tells us how we show that we believe in Christ: "He that hath my commandments, and keepeth them, he it is that loveth me: and he that loveth me shall be loved of my Father, and I will love him, and will manifest myself to him." That is the nametag that will allow us access to heaven. Do we have our identification?

Assurance in My Soul

What assurance I have found in Christ my Saviour!
What a peace He gives to calm my troubled soul.
When I cry to Him, He quickly comes to help me.
I can trust that our great God is in control.

Like an anchor in the sea, Christ holds me steady,
Giving me a sweet assurance in my soul.
Cresting waves shall never cause my faith to waver,
For I trust the risen Christ who makes me whole.

There is nothing like the peace I've found in Jesus;
He has given me a hope steadfast and sure.
He's my Rock, my strong Defense, my mighty Tower;
By His grace, unto the end, I will endure.

And I know that all my sins have been forgiven;
Since I'm bought by God, He won't turn me away.
As His child I have this blessed, sweet salvation,
For He promised He's the Truth, the Life, the Way.

When I'm facing death someday, I'll trust in Jesus,
For His hand will guide me safely in that hour;
Praise the Lord! I know a heavenly home awaits me
When I die, or when Christ comes in all His power.

Jesus gives to all who come a sweet assurance—
We can know that we belong to Him alone
For He bought us with the blood He shed on Calvary;
When He gave His life to purchase back our own.

Consider God's
Wondrous Works

When I was a girl, before the age of air conditioning, my family would often gather on the front porch on hot summer nights to catch a little cool air. As we sat talking, I felt a sense of security, knowing I was surrounded by my parents and siblings. I had no fear of the night. Sometimes a summer storm would blow up and we would see the lightning flash and hear the thunder roll. Then the rain would come. We would marvel at the performance. I never felt any fear of thunderstorms. Although I understand the need of caution, a summer thunderstorm always brings back the memory of my family and me sitting on the porch until the wind drove the rain in on us. Then we would scurry into the house and to bed.

A thunderstorm is one of the many ways God speaks to us of His power, majesty, wisdom, and knowledge. Who can understand the Creator of this universe? Job 37:23 says, "Touching the Almighty, we cannot find him out." Yet, God reveals Himself to us in His creation and in His Word. In Job 38:4–11, we read how God laid the foundations of the earth and how He made boundaries for the seas. He made the rain and caused the tender herb to grow. He made both the snow and the hail. Throughout chapters 38–41, God exposes Job's ignorance of God and His workings, which are past finding out. Today man understands many things about nature, but this knowledge has not, nor will it ever, match the scope of God's limitless wisdom. God controls the universe. He sends the rain, the frost, the snow, and the lightning according to His will.

When I consider the power of God and His sovereignty, I feel a much greater sense of security than I used to feel on the front porch with my family. With God as my heavenly Father, I am safe. Who is greater than our mighty God? As we look at the world around us and consider the handiwork of our eternal God, how can we not give Him all glory and praise?

Praise Him

I ponder God's creation as it speaks its Maker's power;
Yet I can hardly fathom the perfection of a flower,
Each tiny petal nestled in its place within God's bower;
It causes me to praise God's wisdom every single hour.

I hear the rolling thunder and I watch as lightning flashes;
I stand in awe and wonder as the rain in puddles splashes.
These glimpses of the hand of God attune my heart to praising;
But pondering how God loves me is nothing but amazing!

Cleaning House

Some women faithfully deep clean their houses every spring and fall. When we clean thoroughly we usually find things that have been cluttering our living space, things that are useless or broken. Sometimes we find things that we thought were lost. Some items that we no longer use, we still hang onto for sentimental reasons, or because we think we might sometime have a use for them.

The Scripture passage for today tells how King Josiah instigated the cleaning and repairing of the house of the Lord. In the course of their repairing, they found a book which they gave Shaphan, the scribe. After reading it, he showed the book to the king and read it to him. When the king heard the words of the book of the law, he rent his clothes. King Josiah realized that God was angry because they had not been keeping His law. Immediately, he determined to remedy this.

King Josiah gathered the elders of Judah and Jerusalem and read to them the words of the book of the law which had been found in the house of the Lord. Together, they covenanted to walk after the Lord and keep His commandments with all their hearts and with all their souls. Then the king cleansed the temple of vessels that had been made for Baal. He also destroyed the groves where idols were worshiped, getting rid of the idolatrous priests in obedience to the law of God.

Each of us has a house within that we dare not neglect—the heart. We often need to deep clean, asking God to reveal if there is anything within us that He desires to root out. When we open our hearts to God's scrutiny, He may reveal habits or desires that are not pleasing to Him. Are we willing to do as King Josiah did and repent of our sin?

Repentance calls for brokenness before God. Psalm 34:18 says, "The LORD is nigh unto them that are of a broken heart; and saveth such as be of a contrite spirit." Psalm 33:18 tells us, "Behold, the eye of the LORD is upon them that fear him, upon them that hope in his mercy." When God speaks to us about sin, we must heed His voice. Continuing in disobedience will only bring hardness to our hearts and deafness to the voice of the Holy Spirit.

Getting rid of unnecessary or sinful things is a freeing experience, enabling us to have deeper fellowship with our God, become clear witnesses for Him, and be filled with His peace and joy. May we relinquish control of our lives and allow God to reign supreme in our hearts. Only God can deep clean our hearts, making us whiter than snow. Then we can say, "And he hath put a new song in my mouth, even praise unto our God" (Psalm 40:3).

Pleasing Christ

Oh, happy thought, that Christ is here,
He dwells within my heart!
I want to make Him feel at home,
So He will not depart.

And so I'll ask Him every day
To cleanse my heart anew.
I never want to bring Him pain
By sinful things I do.

My fondest wish must be to bring
A gift of love each day,
That I would know I'm pleasing Him,
By what I do and say.

Lord, always stay here in my heart;
May it your temple be;
May all I do bring praise to you,
Through all eternity.

Hidden Things

One of my sons was struggling with his math. Almost every evening I tried to help him, but it still seemed very difficult for him. One day his math book was missing. We all searched for it, but it was not to be found. I had to buy another one so my son could continue his study.

The following spring, I decided to clean out a back storage room, so we moved everything. What a surprise when we discovered my son's missing math book behind a tall workbench. In frustration, my son had hidden his book, thinking he would not have to do it if he did not have a book. Of course, that was not the case.

That incident made me think of Numbers 32:23, "And be sure your sin will find you out." In Joshua 7, we read how Joshua and his men were defeated in battle because of hidden sin. Achan had taken things at the battle of Jericho that he was forbidden to take. He had hidden them in the ground under his tent, but God knew they were there and did not permit them to have victory. Similarly, hidden sin will keep us from spiritual victory. 1 Corinthians 4:5 tells us that when the Lord returns, He will "bring to light the hidden things of darkness, and will make manifest the counsels of the hearts."

Like David, we must acknowledge: "O God, thou knowest my foolishness; and my sins are not hid from thee" (Psalm 69:5). My young son thought his math book was well hidden, but it eventually came to light. So it will be with all those things we might think are hidden. When Christ returns and we face that great Judgment Day, those things will be made evident to all. Remember, God sees them now.

How much better to confess our sins to Christ now, for He has promised to forgive us and cleanse us from all unrighteousness (1 John 1:9). Then we will have peace with Christ. We won't have to worry about hidden things coming to light.

Show Me

Lord, show me my heart; let nothing be hid.
Clean all the corners—I'll do as you bid.

To you I'll submit, my own will to cease,
That glory to you may ever increase.

I long not for power, nor gold of the land,
But peace in my heart as you hold my hand.

Famished or *Filled?*

While reading Proverbs 10, I was struck by verse 3, "The LORD will not suffer the soul of the righteous to famish." *Adam Clarke's Commentary* provides this explanation: "The righteous have God for their feeder; and because of His infinite bounty, they can never famish for want of the bread of life."[3]

When my children arrived home from school, their cries of "I'm famished," "What's to eat?" or "I can't wait for supper!" filled the kitchen. Of course, I gave them something to eat. They knew they could depend on Mom. I was their feeder, even as God is our Feeder.

God provided food for various needy people in Bible times—oil and meal for the widow, food carried by ravens to Elijah, and manna for the Israelites in the wilderness.

My mind mulled over this thought of being famished. I had the picture of someone who had gone so long without eating that his body was desperately in need of food. Then I thought about my soul. Is it well fed with nourishing food? Have I been feasting on the Bread of Life, or is my soul nearly famished because of my neglect?

There is no lack in God's storehouse. It is filled to the brim and overflowing. There is no reason for us to go hungry. We must come to God on a regular basis to obtain the nourishment that we need for our spiritual growth.

In John 6:35, Jesus said, "I am the bread of life: he that cometh to me shall never hunger; and he that believeth on me shall never thirst."

In verses 47, 48, and 51, we read, "Verily, verily, I say unto you, he that believeth on me hath everlasting life. I am that bread of life. I am the living bread which came down from heaven: if any man eat of this bread, he shall live for ever: and the bread that I will give is my flesh, which I will give for the life of the world."

Our every need is met in Jesus, the Bread of Life. We cannot find sustenance for our spiritual life anywhere else. Let's not go hungry. God is our Feeder. Let's go to Him and be filled.

The Living Bread

I have found the Bread of Life to be sufficient.
I was hungry—now my soul is satisfied;
Like the manna God provided in the desert,
Has this Living Bread my every need supplied.

I'm rejoicing in His mercy and provision.
Praise the Lord! I've found in Him my all in all.
He's the only hope of life for weary sinners;
He satisfies the needs of all who call.

Jesus said that those who seek will surely find Him,
He's the Bread, the Life, the Lamb that overcame,
And the only Way that we can enter heaven;
We must come, repent, believe upon His name.

Malnourished

In front of my father-in-law sat a tray of nourishing food. Once again he shook his head saying, "I'm not hungry; I don't want anything." He had just been released from the hospital where he had received treatment for malnourishment. Now, in a nursing home for rehab, he was exhibiting the same behavior which had caused his hospitalization. Since he had dementia and didn't remember when or if he had eaten, his situation was understandable. At eighty-six, his body was slowing down.

His problem was not the scarcity of food, but his refusal to eat what was provided. His predicament reminded me of our spiritual diet. There is plenty of "food" around us, but will it nourish our souls? Today we have so many resources that are good for us: hymn CDs, sermons, revival meetings, and seminars, to name a few. These can stir up our minds, encouraging us to love and serve God.

Sometimes it almost seems we have too many good things to do or too many good places to go. Busyness may cause us to be undernourished. Psalm 81:10 says, "Open thy mouth wide, and I will fill it." Psalm 107:9 tells us, "For he satisfieth the longing soul, and filleth the hungry soul with goodness."

Refusing to eat nutritious foods results in malnourishment. When we feed on God's Word, we will find all we need for our hungry souls. We will find spiritual strength. Although we managed to get my father-in-law to eat a few bites of food, unless he consistently ate enough, he would not regain the ground he had lost. So with us—we need to nourish ourselves with God's Word regularly. We will see the difference in our lives.

In Psalm 119:97, the psalmist exclaims, "O how love I thy law! it is my meditation all the day." In Psalm 119:103, he continues, "How sweet are thy words unto my taste! yea, sweeter than honey to my mouth!" May we not neglect the most important food. If we feed daily on God's Word, our souls will flourish.

Take Time

My life was filled with busyness
From dawn to dark each day,
But all the good things that I did
Squeezed out my time to pray.

Within, my soul grew small and cold,
My words grew cold and sharp;
The smallest things would irritate,
I'd fuss, nitpick, and harp.

And then one day I understood
The reason for my plight—
I'd tried to make it on my own
Without God's guiding light.

I need to read God's Word each day,
I need to stop and pray.
Without the Lord to guide my steps,
I'll surely lose my way.

So, friends, take heed to all I've said,
It is a lesson true—
Do not forget God's daily bread,
It's life and health to you.

The
Chocolate Bar

When she was a little girl, one of my nieces saw someone eating a piece of what appeared to be a yummy chocolate bar. When she asked for some of it, they only chuckled and said, "No, this isn't for little girls." Christi didn't take no for an answer. She watched when others occasionally helped themselves to the chocolate bar. She decided she was going to have some of it too.

One day when no one else was in the kitchen, Christi sneaked the bar out of the refrigerator and consumed a good portion. As she tucked it away rather untidily, she thought, *It wasn't as good as I thought it would be. Certainly, it wasn't as tasty as Grammy's fudge.*

By the time it was discovered that someone had snitched the "chocolate" bar—which was actually Ex-Lax®—my niece was already feeling its effect. The thing that had so enticed her was revealing its true nature. When my sister explained to her daughter that the bar was not candy but medicine for people who needed it, Christi determined they could have their medicine. She had had quite enough of it.

Sometimes the things Satan offers look tantalizing. Remember, though, that they only appear attractive. They will not satisfy our spiritual hunger, but will bring misery to our souls far greater than the discomfort the "chocolate" brought to my niece. Only Jesus can fill the deep longing within each of us.

Matthew 5:6 says, "Blessed are they which do hunger and thirst after righteousness: for they shall be filled." In Colossians 3:2 we read,

"Set your affection on things above, not on things on the earth." Luke 12:32 says, "Fear not, little flock; for it is your Father's good pleasure to give you the kingdom." Just as our earthly father wants to give us good gifts, so does our heavenly Father. All we have to do is ask.

Let's not hanker after an imitation, but choose the real thing. "O taste and see that the LORD is good" (Psalm 34:8). Jesus says in Matthew 6:33, "But seek ye first the kingdom of God, and his righteousness; and all these things shall be added unto you." We will never be disappointed.

> When the world and its allurements
> Beckon you to turn aside,
> Do not let their charms seduce you,
> But in Jesus Christ abide.

I Come to You

Unworthy, Lord, I come to you,
And humbly ask for strength to do
The things you want from me today.
Lord, give me grace to walk your way.

Alone, I cannot face the day;
Temptations sore may come my way.
I need your strength and power within
To keep me from the paths of sin.

Lord, I must run to you in prayer
When burdens hard I'm called to bear.
There's nothing like your tender care,
And knowing you are always there.

Stay close beside me through this day,
And I will try to show the way
To those who cross my path today,
Tell them you are the Truth, the Way.

Whose
Perspective Matters?

If we would survey a cross-section of people, we would likely find as many viewpoints on a subject as we had people. It is human nature to feel our perspective is the right one. In our society today, many people think it is fine for each person to believe in whatever or whomever they please. People promote the philosophy that it does not really matter who, what, or how one worships or believes, believing that all ways lead to God.

As Christians, we believe the Bible is the inerrant Word of God, and is the final authority in all matters. When we cease to hold to this conviction, our faith becomes weak, and our doctrine subject to error. If we deem the Bible a work of man, we deny the power and authority of the immortal God who said, "I am the Alpha and Omega, the first and the last" (Revelation 22:13).

In a day when obtaining a good education is highly esteemed by most, few seek true wisdom. Job asked, "But where shall wisdom be found? and where is the place of understanding?" (Job 28:12). In verses 23, 24, and 28 he answers: "God understandeth the way thereof, and he knoweth the place thereof. For he looketh to the ends of the earth, and seeth under the whole heaven; . . . And unto man he said, Behold, the fear of the Lord, that is wisdom; and to depart from evil is understanding."

Today many voices proclaim, "This is the way." Yet people refuse to acknowledge Jesus as God come in the flesh, or to acknowledge the

God of the Bible as Creator of the universe. They scoff at the idea of future judgment for sin. Each one has a different opinion on what to believe or whether to believe in anything at all.

Psalm 1 gives us God's perspective: "Blessed is the man that walketh not in the counsel of the ungodly, nor standeth in the way of sinners, nor sitteth in the seat of the scornful. But his delight is in the law of the LORD; and in his law doth he meditate day and night" (Psalm 1:1–2). The man who does this shall prosper, but the ungodly will not even be able to stand in the Day of Judgment. In the end, whose perspective really matters? God will have the last word on all things. Blessed are those who put their trust in Him. His Word will endure. "The words of the LORD are pure words: as silver tried in a furnace of earth, purified seven times. Thou shalt keep them, O LORD, thou shalt preserve them from this generation for ever" (Psalm 12:6–7).

May we, with David, cry out to God, "Shew me thy ways, O LORD; teach me thy paths. Lead me in thy truth, and teach me" (Psalm 25:4–5). Psalm 25:8–9 tells us, "Good and upright is the LORD: therefore will he teach sinners in the way. The meek will he guide in judgment: and the meek will he teach his way." Let's humble ourselves before God and learn of Him. May we defer to His perspective in all things, for His is the one that matters.

Keep the Faith

Remember well the saints of old
Those prophets firm and martyrs bold.
From hearts triumphant came their cry,
"Keep the faith; fear not to die!"

What was this faith so dearly bought
That bid them count their lives as nought?
It was the teachings Jesus gave
Before He wrestled with the grave.

Commanded by our blessed Lord
To love our foes, we shun the sword,
And keep unspotted from the world
Though fiery darts at us are hurled.

When all about on every side
Are churches drifting with the tide,
May we His banner gladly fly
With "Keep the faith!" our battle cry.

Part
TWO

Separated
unto God

Babes
in Christ

Standing in the hospital nursery, I listened to the cries of several newborn babies. It was two o'clock in the morning—feeding time. I had already taken the breastfed babies to their mothers. Now the nurse and I would give the other babies their bottles of formula. Finally, all were fed and tucked snugly into their beds. Quietness reigned. The babies slept the sleep of contentment.

1 Peter 2:2 instructs us: "As newborn babes, desire the sincere milk of the word that ye may grow thereby: if so be ye have tasted that the Lord is gracious." It does not take long for newborn babies to desire milk. Their bodies tell them they are hungry, and they are very impatient when it is feeding time. I remember giving a baby his first taste of milk. He was crying furiously, but when that milk dribbled into his mouth, he quieted down and devoted himself to consuming the nourishing milk. It satisfied him.

Like newborns, new Christians should crave the sincere milk of the Word. Reading and studying the Bible is like drinking a tall, cold glass of water or milk on a hot day. It refreshes and nourishes us.

When Paul wrote to the Hebrews, he was concerned that their growth was stunted. Some of them had been Christians for a while, long enough that they should have been able to teach others. Instead, they needed to be taught again the basic doctrines of Christ. Paul told them they ". . . are become such as have need of milk, and not of strong meat. For every one that useth milk is unskillful in the word of righteousness: for he is a babe" (Hebrews 5:12–13).

In the hospital where I worked, we had a nursery where newborn babies were kept who would be adopted. One baby stayed there until she was big enough to pull herself up in the crib. That baby was not content anymore with just milk. We fed her cereal and, later, baby food. Similarly, as newborn Christians, we should be growing on the "milk of the Word." Eventually, we should become hungry for the "meat of the Word." This is what Paul desired for the Hebrews.

In the book of Hebrews, Paul shows how Christ and His priesthood are better than the Old Testament law and its priesthood. Hebrews is known as the book of better things. Paul whets the appetites of young Christians. To really feed on meat, we need to pray, asking God for understanding of His Word. We need to read and study it often. We must apply it to our lives, asking how it affects our daily choices. Does my thinking conform to the Word? How can I further the kingdom of God? How can I be an asset to my church or a help to my neighbor? God wants His Word to become a part of us, not just a book we read. Then we will grow into the mature Christians He wants us to be, Christians who will produce fruit to glorify His name.

Come Closer

Are you walking with the Saviour
In sweet fellowship each day,
Finding joy in daily living
In the straight and narrow way?

Are you feasting on His manna,
Finding treasures rich and rare?
Are you finding Christ is dearer,
With each blessed hour of prayer?

Or have you His Word neglected,
Found your prayer time rather slim?
Have you lost that fervent spirit?
Has your joy in Christ grown dim?

Hear the Saviour; He is calling,
"Come still closer to my side."
If you long for close communion,
You must in the Lord abide.

Transformed

*T*oday's scripture talks about two blind men sitting by the wayside as Jesus and His disciples departed from Jericho. They were beggars, dependent on the mercy of others for their living. When they heard that Jesus was passing by, they cried out, "Have mercy on us, O Lord, thou Son of David" (Matthew 20:30). The crowd rebuked them, telling them to hold their peace. Did this stop them? No, for these men had a great need. Were they going to be quiet when healing was so near? No, they cried out all the more until Jesus stood still and asked them, "What will ye that I shall do unto you?" (20:32). The men replied, "Lord, that our eyes may be opened" (20:33).

These men were persistent because they believed that Jesus could restore their sight. They were rewarded for their faith. Matthew 20:34 says, "So Jesus had compassion on them, and touched their eyes: and immediately their eyes received sight, and they followed him." Jesus transformed their lives. They no longer had to beg by the wayside. They were healed, and now they had a mission. They became followers of Jesus.

Another time Jesus and His disciples met a man who lived among the tombs in the country of the Gadarenes (Luke 8:26–27). This man was uncontrollable. He cried and cut himself with stones. Strong chains could not hold him. The unclean spirits within the man recognized Jesus as the Son of God. When Jesus commanded the demons to leave the man, He allowed them to go into a herd of swine nearby. When they did so, the herd of two thousand ran headlong into the sea and was drowned.

When the keepers of the swine came to see what had happened, they found the man who had been naked and uncontrollable, sitting clothed and in his right mind. He didn't cry out or cut himself anymore. He was calm and at peace. He had been transformed! The keepers were afraid, for they had seen the power of God. They wanted Jesus to get out of their country. In contrast, the man who had been delivered wanted to follow Jesus wherever He went. However, Jesus gave him a mission. He told the man to stay in his own country, go home to his friends, and tell them what great things the Lord had done for him and what compassion Jesus had had on him. Jesus asked that transformed man to become a missionary.

When we experience the power of Jesus Christ in our lives, acknowledging Him as Lord, we, too, are transformed. Our goals and desires are different. We have a mission—to serve Jesus Christ. We want to walk with Him. We want to tell others what He has done for us, and of His great compassion for sinners. Can others see the transforming power of Jesus Christ in our lives?

Transformed by Christ

I watched as the desolate, muddy land
Was covered by sparkling, frosty snow.
Transformed was the wilderness that I knew
To a breathtaking view that glowed.

I thought of the barrenness of my soul,
The blackness of sin in my burdened heart
Till Christ in His graciousness reached within,
And He gave me a newborn start.

His blood, like the snow, covered all my sins,
As deep as the stains on the ground below.
I've been purified from the inside out,
Even whiter than spotless snow.

A Holy

People

When God called Abram to leave his home and kindred and to journey to a land that He would show him, He promised that Abram would become a great nation (Genesis 12:2). Through him, all the nations of the earth would be blessed. Sometime later, God told Abram, "Walk before me, and be thou perfect" (Genesis 17:1). God changed his name to Abraham, marking a new beginning in his life. The new nation of God's holy people had been born.

Later, as Moses led the children of Israel from Egypt to the land of Canaan, God gave them commandments concerning the nations they would drive out of Canaan. God commanded the Israelites not to make any covenants or marriages with these people, but to utterly destroy them. The reason was that they were to be ". . . an holy people unto the LORD thy God" (Deuteronomy 7:6). They were to be set apart for Him.

Deuteronomy 14:2 further emphasizes, "For thou art an holy people unto the LORD thy God, and the LORD hath chosen thee to be a peculiar people unto himself, above all the nations that are upon the earth."

Mankind, however, cannot attain holiness on his own. Romans 3:10 tells us, "As it is written, There is none righteous, no, not one," and in verse 12, "There is none that doeth good, no, not one." Romans 3:23 declares, "For all have sinned, and come short of the glory of God."

How then can we be the holy people God calls us to be?

Isaiah 45:22 commands, "Look unto me, and be ye saved, all the ends of the earth: for I am God, and there is none else." God so loved us that He sent His Son to die for us, to become the propitiation for our sins. When we believe in Christ Jesus, the Son of God, we are justified, forgiven, and made righteous. We cannot make ourselves holy, but God can. To be *holy* is to be "chaste, spotless, pure, clean, sanctified, and consecrated to God."[4]

Holiness is emphasized throughout the Scriptures, for God is a holy God who demands no less of His people. We cannot flirt with the world and be separated unto God.

In Revelation 4:8, we are again reminded of God's holiness. In heaven the four beasts rest neither day nor night, but continually cry, "Holy, holy, holy, Lord God Almighty, which was, and is, and is to come."

Revelation 19:8 describes the bride of Christ, the church. She has prepared herself to meet Christ, her bridegroom. She has been given fine linen, clean and white, to wear. This is the robe of righteousness which Christ gives us when we are cleansed through His blood. It is not our robe of righteousness, but that which Christ gives us. His bride must be found pure, spotless, and undefiled.

In our reading for today, we are reminded that we were not redeemed by corruptible things like silver or gold, but with the precious blood of Christ. He is our only claim to holiness. Without faith in Christ, we cannot be the holy people of God; with Him there is mercy, grace, and power to be holy. Praise, honor, and glory to the Lamb!

The Lamb of God

Oh, see the Lamb, the Son of God
Upon a cross of shame;
The One who took for us that day
Our sin, and all our blame.

Behold, His hands, His feet, His brow;
He loved this world, and gave
His very life and blood for us,
And every sin forgave.

All we like sheep have gone astray,
And hopeless would we be,
Had not the Shepherd good and kind,
Spent all for you and me.

What can we say if we refuse
The gift of love Christ bought?
How can we turn our hearts away
From what our God has wrought?

Oh, fall upon your knees today,
Confess Him full and free;
There is no other love like His,
Nor ever will there be.

A Living Sacrifice

What does it mean to *sacrifice?* The dictionary defines it as "giving up something valuable or important for somebody or something else that is considered of more value or importance."[5] In Romans 12:1, Paul encourages the believers to give themselves in service to God, laying down their own desires and plans. God's plans are surely more important than our own. In the light of the sacrifice He made for us, how can we hesitate to give our all for Him?

Those who have laid down their physical lives for Christ we call *martyrs.* They remained faithful to God even when the enemies of the Gospel of Jesus Christ persecuted and killed them. This is true sacrifice, giving up our mortal life for God's sake. But God calls us to living martyrdom—to lay down our lives daily as living sacrifices for Him. How do we do this?

Paul describes one way in Romans 1:16: "For I am not ashamed of the gospel of Christ: for it is the power of God unto salvation to everyone that believeth." Being willing to stand for Christ in every situation, unashamed to call Him Lord before everyone, regardless of the cost, is part of being a living sacrifice for Christ.

In the Old Testament when an animal was sacrificed, it had to be clean. That is, according to the ceremonial law, it could have been used for food. It had to be free of disease or imperfections. It was set aside as holy unto the Lord. Similarly, God calls us to a life of holiness, consecrated to Him. Romans 12:9 commands, "Abhor that which is evil;

cleave to that which is good."

What makes our sacrifice acceptable to God? Romans 14:17–18 tells us, "The kingdom of God is not meat and drink; but righteousness, and peace, and joy in the Holy Ghost. For he that in these things serveth Christ is acceptable to God, and approved of men." In the next verse, Paul tells us to pursue peace and that which will edify each other. If we try to do the work of God but are not at peace with our brother or sister, our efforts are not acceptable to God.

We must remember that our righteousness is found in Christ alone. Only through Him can we be acceptable. Only by His power can we follow the admonition given in Romans 12:2. If our hearts are set on the things of this world, we will not be able to present ourselves as living sacrifices unto God. To live the way Christ expects us to, our minds must be renewed by Him.

Jesus tells us in Matthew 6:19–21 not to lay up treasures on this earth. The things of this earth cannot have first place in our lives if we are to be living sacrifices for God. Instead, the deeds we do, the life we live, must be for eternity. If we live for self, we cannot lay up treasures in heaven.

Presenting our bodies as a living sacrifice to God will not always feel pleasant to the flesh. When they were beaten, the apostles rejoiced that they were counted worthy to suffer shame for Christ's name (Acts 5:41). We, too, should count it all joy to give ourselves to the service of Christ, even when it involves suffering.

Commitment

Do we seek an easy road
With no heavy cross to bear?
Do we want to enter heaven,
Never having suffered here?

Jesus said, "Take up your cross;
Leave your nets and follow me."
Then He walked the Calvary road;
Will we follow where He leads?

Will we bear the scorn and hate,
Count it joy to share the shame
That is ours because we're true
To our Lord's most holy name?

If we give our life to Christ,
All our will to Him lay down,
Bear the cross and walk the road,
We shall wear the victor's crown.

A Willing *Heart*

God instructed Moses to erect a tabernacle for Him. Moses summoned the entire congregation to a special meeting to hear the instructions which God had given him. To begin the construction of the tabernacle, materials were needed. Those who were able to contribute and who had a willing heart were told to bring their offerings.

Men and women alike contributed to the project. Some brought expensive gifts of gold, silver, brass, or precious stones. Some brought the wood that was needed. Those who had rams' skins and badgers' skins offered them. Others gave spices and oil for the incense. Still others volunteered their skills. Exodus 35:25–26 tells us, "All the women that were wise hearted did spin with their hands, and brought that which they had spun, both of blue, and of purple, and of scarlet, and of fine linen. And all the women whose heart stirred them up in wisdom spun goats' hair."

Verse 29 underscores that this offering was a willing offering. The people's hearts were stirred to give. No gift was esteemed greater than another. Each unique contribution was needed for God's tabernacle. Each gift was important. God wanted each person to feel that his contribution was vital to the work. It was to be the work of them all. Over and over God reminded them that it was to be a willing offering. When we give out of a sense of obligation, we miss the blessing of giving willingly. Whether we give money, time, or talents, we must give it with a willing heart.

We must never excuse ourselves by saying that we have nothing to give. Some people say, "I don't have any talents." All God desires is a willing heart that is moved to help, willing to be used in whatever way God chooses. What a beautiful church is built when each one gives willingly! Even the prayers that are offered are sweet incense ascending to God above.

The children of Israel brought freewill offerings every morning until one day the leaders came to Moses and said, "The people bring much more than enough for the service of the work" (Exodus 36:5). So Moses announced that no more offerings were needed. The people had to be held back from giving.

Psalm 96:8 says, "Give unto the LORD the glory due unto his name: bring an offering, and come into his courts." God wants our offerings today. He wants us to offer ourselves to Him and to His service. Will we joyfully and willingly give Him our very best—our all? May our hearts be stirred to give.

A Willing Offering

A willing offering now we bring
To you, our Lord and King,
To honor and adore your name
And praise you as we sing.

Our hearts and minds, our strength we give,
In all sincerity,
To serve you with a heart of love,
For you have set us free.

Our lives we offer willingly,
We lay them at your feet;
Our highest praise, our deepest love
Is yours alone, complete.

A Peculiar Treasure

*M*any families have special heirlooms. One of my husband's special treasures is an antique clock that belonged to his great-grandfather. He grew up hearing it chime at his grandparents' house, so he was thrilled when they gave it to him. Regardless of its monetary value, it holds great sentimental worth to my husband. It brings back happy memories of yesteryear.

Genesis 12 records how God called Abraham to leave his home and follow God to a land that He would give him. God promised to bless all the nations of the world through Abraham's family. Abraham waited until he was one hundred years old for God to give him the promised son, Isaac, through whom God would make a great nation. God made a covenant with Abraham saying, "Walk before me, and be thou perfect" (Genesis 17:1).

Years later, three months after Moses had led them out of Egypt, the Israelites were camped in the wilderness of Sinai. God spoke to Moses telling him to give the Israelites this message: "Ye have seen what I did unto the Egyptians, and how I bare you on eagles' wings, and brought you to myself. Now therefore, if ye will obey my voice indeed, and keep my covenant, then ye shall be a peculiar treasure unto me above all people: for all the earth is mine: And ye shall be unto me a kingdom of priests, and an holy nation" (Exodus 19:4–6).

God wanted this people for a peculiar treasure, but there was a condition they had to meet. They had to obey Him and worship Him alone.

He could not overlook their disobedience or their idolatry. When they forsook Him, He punished them, reprimanding them for their sins.

How it must have hurt the heart of God to see His special treasure flaunting their sins before His holy eyes! Eventually, their disobedience caused them to be scattered among many countries for a time. God still longed for a people wholly dedicated to Him. To redeem the world back to Himself, He sent His only begotten Son, Jesus. Now the way was opened, not only for the Jews, but also for the Gentiles to become His peculiar treasure. Paul instructed Titus to reprove sharply those who professed to know God, but whose actions showed otherwise (Titus 1:13–16). God's standard has never changed. Titus 2:12 tells us to live "soberly, righteously, and godly." If we do this, we can be part of His special treasure.

Titus 2:13 tells us how Christ, our Redeemer, will return for His people. In Revelation 5:9–10 the prophecy of Exodus 19:6—that God would call out for Himself a kingdom of priests—is fulfilled as Jesus takes the book with seven seals. The twenty-four elders fall down before the Lamb, singing a new song, "Thou art worthy to take the book, and to open the seals thereof: for thou was slain, and hast redeemed us to God by thy blood out of every kindred, and tongue, and people, and nation; And hast made us unto our God kings and priests: and we shall reign on the earth" (Revelation 5:9–10).

God calls these people His peculiar treasure. They are redeemed by Jesus' blood, and belong exclusively to Him. Will we be among this number? God wants us for His special treasure.

Entirely His

God wants a holy people,
Exclusively His own,
The ones who follow Jesus
And worship Him alone.

God wants our hearts entirely,
Our love without reserve;
He says we must obey Him
And all His ways observe.

God's own peculiar treasure
He'll gather home someday.
Will you be in that number?
Believe on Christ today.

A Vacant Lot

Many people see a vacant lot as an invitation to litter. No one is too concerned about what happens to it. Similarly, a vacant, purposeless mind is an invitation for Satan to drop trash there. Perhaps the writer of Proverbs 4:23 was conscious of this when he wrote, "Keep thy heart with all diligence; for out of it are the issues of life." If we do not fill our minds with God's Word, His songs, and good things, the devil will take the opportunity to drop in some bad words, ungodly songs, or impure thoughts.

We used to have a goat that was a favorite of our youngest son Nathan. That goat was not choosy about what she ate. She would even eat paper or my flowers if she could get to them. One time when Nathan was standing near her, she plucked his straw hat off his head and ate the whole thing.

Some people are like that. They feed their minds indiscriminately on whatever is within reach whether it is good for them or not. Soon their minds become like a vacant lot, littered with decaying trash.

Luke 6:45 tells us that what is within is made known: "A good man out of the good treasure of his heart bringeth forth that which is good; and an evil man out of the evil treasure of his heart bringeth forth that which is evil: for of the abundance of the heart his mouth speaketh."

What is in our minds will come out in the form of actions and words. We must not allow ourselves to become dumping stations for Satan's trash. Instead, let's be filled with the Spirit of God, feasting on good things that will edify our souls. May we follow the admonition found in Philippians 4:8, "Finally, brethren, whatsoever things are true, whatsoever things are honest, whatsoever things are just, whatsoever things are pure, whatsoever things are lovely, whatsoever things are of good report; if there be any virtue, and if there be any praise, think on these things."

May our heart cry be that of David in Psalm 19:14: "Let the words of my mouth, and the meditation of my heart, be acceptable in thy sight, O LORD, my strength, and my redeemer."

What Are We Thinking?

Throughout the hours of daily life, our minds flit here and there;
We think of things that we must do, our duties to complete;
We wonder if we'll have the time to read, or sew, or shop;
And what our friends are doing now, and what we'll fix to eat.

But down below the surface look—just what do we see there?
Is what our minds are dwelling on fit for our Lord to see?
What are the things we feed upon? Do they breed good or ill?
If they were clear for all to see, what would the record be?

Our thoughts, before they're even formed, are known by Christ our Lord;
We cannot hide a thing from Him; our minds are His to see.
If we will ask the Lord to cleanse our hearts of carnal things,
And concentrate on noble things, our lives will blessed be.

Accepting
My Place

We had been married only a few months when my husband came to me, Bible in hand. "I've been studying 1 Corinthians 11, and I think you should start covering your head for church," he said.

"Oh, really?" I replied. "Well, I have a couple of hats. I guess I could wear one of them."

"No," he said, "I think it should be something especially made for prayer."

I looked at him incredulously. "You mean like the Amish or something?"

"Yeah, I guess so," he answered.

"Well, I don't know. How about letting me study this for myself first?" He agreed, and my search into God's design for headship began.

The first thing I discovered is that God is a God of order. Throughout Scripture, God demonstrates that He is supreme. There is no one higher than Him. The second thing I noticed is that Jesus, God's only begotten Son, is second in command. Though Christ is equal to God in who He is and what He can do, Christ always defers to the Father. (For example, see John 14:10.)

God made man from the dust of the earth and breathed into him the breath of life. He created man in His own image. The third principle about God's order of authority is that man is to be subordinate to Christ. Then in 1 Corinthians 11:3, I confronted the clear words:

"The head of the woman is the man." Ephesians 5:22–24 confirms this: "Wives, submit yourselves unto your own husbands, as unto the Lord. For the husband is the head of the wife, even as Christ is the head of the church." 1 Peter 3:1 also speaks of wives submitting to their husbands.

1 Corinthians 11:4 says that when a man prays with his head covered, he dishonors his head, or Christ. When a woman prays with her head uncovered, however, she dishonors man or her husband, who is her head. For her to pray or prophesy (testify) with her head uncovered is as if she were shaven. Verse 6 suggests it is a shame for a woman to have her hair cut off or shaved. In Jeremiah 7:29, Jeremiah cried, "Cut off thine hair, O Jerusalem, and cast it away." Because Israel had committed gross sins but still maintained a semblance of worship to God, God pronounced judgment on her. Jeremiah's metaphor, the call to cut off her hair, demonstrated her degradation and separation from God. Cutting off her hair was a symbol of shame. Thus it is a shame for woman to be without the natural glory that God gave her. Refusing to take our place in subjection to man is direct disobedience to God, for He is the one who set up the headship order.

Why is it difficult to accept wearing a veiling or covering on our heads? First, it can be humbling. It sets us apart from other women in society. I remember the remarks made by our families when I began to wear one. Furthermore, it is a daily reminder that we are to submit to our husbands. Accepting that place means surrendering ourselves to the will of God.

1 Corinthians 11:9–10 seems to imply that even the angels take notice of the woman's veiling. May we joyfully accept our place in the headship order, and gladly cover our heads to declare our submission to God's design.

Let Her Be Veiled

"Let her be veiled," the Scriptures say
Let man direct instead;
The angels look from heaven and see
The power on her head.

Submission is a lovely thing
When from the heart it springs;
Contentment's but a hidden joy
That moves the heart to sing.

May my behavior harmonize
With my submission sign;
The veil that rests upon my head
Speak of a heart resigned.

Call to
Commitment

One thing an employer values about an employee is his commitment. Does he show up on time every day? Does he do his work thoroughly whether someone is watching or not? Is he loyal to the company, obedient to the rules? Does he get along well with others? Does he recommend the company to others?

Jesus also wants our commitment. He wants us to be "on time," ready to serve when He calls. In Matthew 4:18–20, Jesus was walking by the Sea of Galilee when he saw two brothers, Peter and Andrew, who were fishing. He said to them, "Follow me, and I will make you fishers of men" (Matthew 4:19). The next verse says, "And they straightway left their nets, and followed him." As they left, Jesus saw two more brothers, James and John, who were in a ship with their father, mending their nets. When Jesus called them, they immediately left the ship and their father and followed Him (Matthew 4:21). Are we available when Christ calls us to serve? Have we left all to follow Christ?

Can Christ depend on us to do our best whether or not anyone is watching? Jesus condemned the scribes and Pharisees, saying, "But all their works they do for to be seen of men" (Matthew 23:5). Christ wants His followers to be faithful at all times, not just when people are watching.

Christ demands our loyalty. We cannot live for Him and for the world and Satan at the same time. Matthew 6:24 declares, "No man can serve two masters: for either he will hate the one, and love the other; or else he will hold to the one, and despise the other. Ye cannot serve God and mammon."

In the workplace there are rules to follow. So it is with Christ. He wants our obedience to His rules or commandments. John 14:15 says, "If ye love me, keep my commandments." Verse 21 enlarges on this thought: "He that hath my commandments, and keepeth them, he it is that loveth me: and he that loveth me shall be loved of my Father, and I will love him, and will manifest myself to him." Our obedience will be rewarded with a fuller knowledge of Christ.

Jesus also calls us to get along with one another. John 13:35 records Jesus' words: "By this shall all men know that ye are my disciples, if ye have love one to another." John 15:13 shows us the measure of true love: "Greater love hath no man than this, that a man lay down his life for his friends."

An employer's purpose in hiring someone is to have that person's work bring profit to the company. If he does not do this, he is a useless employee and will probably be fired. Christ has chosen us to be workers for Him. John 15:16 tells us, "Ye have not chosen me, but I have chosen you, and ordained you, that ye should go and bring forth fruit." To be committed to Christ, we must do as Jesus said: "Thou shalt love the Lord thy God with all thy heart, and with all thy soul, and with all thy mind" (Matthew 22:37). When we do this, commitment will not be difficult, but a joy. Remember, we are serving the King of kings! We will gladly recommend Jesus to the whole world, for He is worthy!

His Call, Our Commitment

When Jesus called the fishermen,
"Come now and follow me,"
They dropped their nets, forsaking all,
His followers to be.

They left their business by the sea;
With fishing they were done.
They had no time for boats and nets;
They had a race to run.

The Master still sends out the call,
"Will you come follow me?"
And still He asks us for our all;
Will we give willingly?

The labor may be long and hard,
We'll work, come rain or sun;
Yet, in the end, we'll smile and rest
When Jesus says, "Well done."

Scripture reading: John 12:44–50

Choices

Every day we make choices: what shoes to wear, which sweater to put on with this dress, what kind of car to buy, or which neighborhood to live in. When my two oldest sons were young, the older son would wear whatever I chose for him each day. The younger, however, had opinions. Some people allow others to make choices for them. Sometimes the choice is insignificant. A year from now it will make little difference whether someone buys us a fish sandwich when we really wanted a hamburger.

Other choices in life are too important to leave to others. Choosing a career is a major decision. Choosing a life companion is an even weightier one. How can we be sure we are making the right choices in life? The answer to this involves another choice we need to make. It is the most important choice we will make in our entire lives. This choice affects every aspect of our lives now and throughout eternity.

Jesus Christ asks us to believe in Him. We have a choice to make. Will we believe that Christ is indeed the Son of the living God? John 3:36 tells us: "He that believeth on the Son hath everlasting life: and he that believeth not the Son shall not see life; but the wrath of God abideth on him."

Jesus asks us to make a choice. Will we choose life or death? Although many choices we make do not matter too much one way or another, this choice has eternal consequences. What a sobering thought.

Christ offers us so much: a clean, pure heart, our sins forgiven and forgotten, peace of mind, joy, and His presence within us. If we do not choose Christ, we face a lifetime of emptiness and a hopeless eternity.

There are those who question whether there is any existence after death; their doubts do not change the truth of God's eternal Word. Romans 6:23 says, "For the wages of sin is death; but the gift of God is eternal life through Jesus Christ our Lord."

Christ chose to obey His Father to come to earth and do the work He was called to do. When Christ freely gave His life on the cross, He did so because we needed a Saviour to rescue us from our sins. We can never be good enough on our own to merit heaven. We needed Christ to shed His blood for us and to vanquish death through His resurrection. He died so we can live; but it is our choice whether or not we accept His redemption. Will we choose life today? May we say as Joshua did, "But as for me and my house, we will serve the LORD" (Joshua 24:15).

The Crossroad

A crossroad in life lies before us;
We all have a choice we must make.
Our destiny lies in the choosing;
Which way, oh my friend, will you take?

The devil displays his enticements;
"Come now, and enjoy life today;
I'll give to you pleasure and riches."
But oh, what a price you will pay.

The Saviour is calling the drifters,
"Come now, and believe I'm the way."
Each one must decide whom he'll follow,
Whose voice he will choose to obey.

When crossroads in life we encounter,
There's always a choice we must make;
One way leads to life with our Saviour
And one to the sulfurous lake.

Who Are You?

When a person wants to obtain a driver's license or make changes on it, he must produce several forms of identification to prove that he is who he says he is. Those in authority examine his papers to verify his identity. Sometimes identity theft occurs where someone steals another person's information and claims it as his own. I read once of a man who wanted to impersonate another man. The two men had a lot of similarities, but one was left-handed. For months the first man practiced using his left hand until he could use it naturally. Although he looked and acted like the other man, he was an imposter. Inside, he was still himself. Though man can be fooled, God cannot. God knows who we are deep inside, no matter who we may pretend to be on the outside.

The Bible records that Jesus called some people *hypocrites*. The dictionary defines *hypocrite* as: "someone who gives a false appearance of having admirable principles, beliefs, or feelings."[6]

In Matthew 6:1–4, Jesus instructed His disciples about giving alms, telling them to do it without drawing attention to themselves as the hypocrites did. He also told them that when they prayed, they should go to a private place, unlike the hypocrites who liked to pray in the synagogues or on the street corners so that others would see them and think how holy they must be.

Jesus warned His disciples of the leaven of the Pharisees, which is hypocrisy. He reminded them, "There is nothing covered, that shall not be revealed; neither hid, that shall not be known" (Luke 12:2–3). Even the things spoken in darkness, in closets, or whispered in the ear will be revealed.

When we do a kind deed, are we eager to let others know? When we give to a needy cause, do we hope others notice how large a sum we give? Do we always want to be in a position of leadership so others will see the good job we do? What motivates our hearts? Are we motivated by the love of Christ within us, or do we, like the Pharisees, want the glory of men? Who are we? What does God see when He looks into our hearts?

In Psalm 51:7, 10, David prays this prayer, "Purge me with hyssop, and I shall be clean: wash me, and I shall be whiter than snow. Create in me a clean heart, O God; and renew a right spirit within me." In verse 17, he tells us what God desires of us: "The sacrifices of God are a broken spirit: a broken and a contrite heart, O God, thou wilt not despise." If there is any hypocrisy in our lives, we must acknowledge it to God. He will cleanse us and give us a right spirit so we will do all things for His glory and honor. Let's not be imposters, but true servants of Jesus Christ.

We Come

Unworthy people, Lord, we come
Before you once again
To ask for mercy for the day,
And power to conquer sin.

Ungrateful children though we are,
Yet still you hear our pleas,
You bless us with your faithfulness;
We bow on humble knees.

Forgive us now as we draw nigh,
And send the grace we need;
For we are helpless people, Lord,
Without you, lost indeed.

For all your goodness, Lord, we bring
Our praises to you now.
With humble, contrite hearts we come,
And low before you bow.

Accept our gifts, O Lord, we pray,
Though little they may seem.
It's all that we can offer you—
The hearts that you've redeemed.

Christmas
in My Heart

Christmas Day, and we were alone. Our families lived five hours away. We had decided it was better not to go home for Christmas since we were expecting the birth of our second child in a couple of weeks. But it was difficult to be separated from our loved ones at this special time of year.

My thoughts went to the first Christmas. I don't know how long it took Joseph and Mary to make the journey from Nazareth to Bethlehem, but I could certainly sympathize with Mary, who was great with child. I imagine Joseph let Mary ride the donkey, but the seventy-five miles still must have been an exhausting journey. How disappointing to find no lodging available except a lowly stable.

The time had come for Mary to deliver her child, and they were alone. There was no family to assist them or even congratulate them. God, however, proclaimed the news to lowly shepherds in a field nearby watching their sheep. The sky shone as a shining angel announced, "Fear not: for, behold, I bring you good tidings of great joy, which shall be to all people. For unto you is born this day in the city of David a Saviour, which is Christ the Lord" (Luke 2:10–11). The angel went on to tell the shepherds where to find the baby.

Suddenly a multitude of the heavenly host appeared with the angel. They were praising God, saying, "Glory to God in the highest, and on earth peace, good will toward men" (Luke 2:14). When the angels vanished from sight, the shepherds decided to see for themselves if the angel's message was true. They hurried into Bethlehem and did indeed find the baby lying in a manger. They left to spread the news of what they had seen and heard; but Mary kept all these things, and pondered them in her heart.

I am sure Mary recalled the angel who had appeared to her and told her she would bear a child who would be the Son of God. When she visited her cousin Elizabeth, she had prophesied, praising God for what He would do for His people through the child she would bear. On this exciting day, perhaps she remembered these things and wondered what lay ahead for this special child.

Christmas is not about family gatherings, gifts, or good food. Christmas is about Christ. It is a time to remember, to worship, and to bring our gifts of love to Christ. Yes, my husband, son, and I were alone that year, and yet, we were not alone. Christ was with us. As we read the story of Jesus' birth, we rejoiced that God had sent such a wonderful gift down to this earth. Although we are unworthy, yet because of His love, God sent His only begotten Son to die for us.

One day Mary understood the great gift her Son is to the world. She watched Him die on the cross, sorrow piercing her soul. She must have rejoiced with the others when she heard that Christ had risen from the dead. Her heart was full of praise and gratefulness to have been a part of God's plan. Wherever we are, whatever the circumstances, we can know we are not alone. Christmas is within our hearts if we believe that Jesus is the Son of God and trust Him to give us everlasting life. We can experience the joy of Christmas every day.

My Christmas Joy

I hurried here and scurried there
To parties almost everywhere;

I shopped, and hoped I had not missed
That someone on my Christmas list.

The cookies, cakes, and popcorn balls,
The pies, and candies—made them all,

For everything must be just right;
I worked and planned with all my might.

I swept, and made my house so clean
That every floor and cupboard gleamed;

I sewed up garments for each one;
I stayed up late till all was done.

I had no time to stop and pray,
Or read of that first Christmas day;

I pushed the children all away;
I had no time to laugh or play.

At last the special day was here;
I wished each one glad Christmas cheer,

But when I paused, I gave a start!
I felt so empty in my heart.

The food was gone, the garments soiled,
The house cluttered over which I'd toiled,

The children fought over each new toy
Till I could not the day enjoy.

At last the children were in bed,
The last goodbyes had all been said;

I dropped into a favorite chair,
Surveying chaos everywhere.

"Is this what Christmas is?" I sighed;
My heart gave out an anguished cry,

"I wanted peace, and joy, and rest;
I wanted to feel loved and blessed."

And then amid the quiet that reigned,
I thought I heard a sweet refrain;

A heavenly choir began to sing,
"Come now and worship Christ the King!"

Then spoke a voice so kind and true,
"My weary child, I died for you.

"Give first place in your heart to me,
And you will find the joy you seek."

I bowed my head, and gave Him all,
And marveled that this act so small

Could fill my heart with peace and joy;
At last I found my Christmas joy.

Where Hate
Is Found

Have you ever heard, or said, "I just can't abide that person," or "I hate liver?" Sometimes we use the words *dislike* and *hate* too loosely. Maybe it is not the person we cannot abide, but his or her ways. Perhaps even the person who hates liver might find it palatable if he or she were hungry enough.

Hate expresses strong feelings of dislike. Intense dislike often seeks an outlet that ends in tragedy. The Bible tells us that he who hates his brother is a murderer (1 John 3:15). Many times hatred, if allowed to grow, will escalate until it culminates in murder.

In today's reading, we see a father who showed favoritism among his children. Joseph's brothers knew their father loved Joseph best. As a token of his preference for Joseph, Jacob gave him a special coat of many colors. Furthermore, Joseph had told his brothers how he dreamed that someday they would bow down to him. Jealousy smoldered within their hearts until it turned to hatred. Genesis 37:4 says they hated Joseph so much that they "could not speak peaceably unto him."

The brothers' hatred nearly ended in murder, but at the last moment, they decided to sell Joseph instead. (Later in the story, we find that this was God's intervention for their salvation.) When hatred is fed, it grows, and there is no telling how far that sin will take us. I have seen it separate families until brothers would not speak to each other.

Adam and Eve's eldest son, Cain, allowed jealousy and hatred to fester in his heart toward his brother Abel. He was not willing to admit his own disobedience, but concentrated on what he perceived as God's partiality toward Abel. These thoughts persisted until Cain killed Abel. Cain even dared to lie to God when God asked him, "Where is Abel thy brother?" (Genesis 4:9).

Consider the example of the twin brothers, Jacob and Esau. Jacob was crafty, and Esau was negligent, a slave of his appetites and lusts. In his hunger, Esau sold his birthright to his brother Jacob for a mess of pottage—a humble bowl of lentils. Later, when Jacob deceived their father and received the blessing in place of Esau, Esau was furious. He threatened that after his father's death he would kill Jacob. He fed his hatred with thoughts of revenge. Their mother quickly sent Jacob away, afraid she would lose both of her sons (Genesis 27:43–45).

Hatred is one of the works of the flesh listed in Galatians 5:19–21. Those who do such things shall not inherit the kingdom of God. Thanks to God, we do not have to succumb to the lusts of the flesh; through Christ, we can find power to be overcomers and walk in the Spirit. God wants us to produce good fruit to the edifying of the body of Christ, and for the good of our own souls. Let's never allow the seeds of hatred and envy to grow in our hearts. We must ask Jesus to cleanse us and keep us walking in the Spirit in righteousness and true holiness.

Seeds

The seeds of hate and envy,
When left to sprout and grow,
Bring forth a fruit ungodly.
We reap what we have sown.

We cannot hate our brother
And love our God above.
The sin of hate is murder,
And Jesus said to love.

We cannot hold within us
The seeds of wrath or strife.
Like bitterness they'll flourish,
Take over all our life.

We need to call on Jesus,
Let Him root out the sin,
So seeds of love and kindness
Can grow and bloom within.

Forgiveness

One Sunday morning one of our sons was unkind to his brother. We admonished him to ask his brother for forgiveness, but he refused to say he was sorry. Instead, he warned, "Dad, we're going to be late for church." He wanted to put off doing what he knew he needed to do. His dad talked to him some more. After he admitted he had been in the wrong, he was willing to tell his brother he was sorry. Forgiveness was granted, and peace reigned.

Isn't forgiveness a beautiful word? How often we need forgiveness from our family, our friends, and most of all, from our Lord. Sometimes we struggle to forgive someone. How does it affect us when we hold a grudge? It makes us miserable, doesn't it?

Peter once asked Jesus how many times a day he should forgive someone. Jesus replied, "Seventy times seven," making it clear that no matter how many times someone sins against us, we must forgive them (Matthew 18:22). We have no other option if we want to receive our heavenly Father's forgiveness.

How often do we think, "It would be easier to forgive if our offender did this or that?" How dare we place conditions on forgiveness?

In Genesis 50:15–18, we read how Joseph's brothers asked him to forgive their cruelty against him. They even declared they would be his servants. Did Joseph rejoice, thinking, *That's just what they deserve for selling me into slavery?* No, Joseph fully forgave them, even promising to care for them and their families.

What happens to our relationship with our heavenly Father when we refuse to forgive others? It is not so easy to talk to Him, is it? Our unforgiving attitude always crops up in our minds. We lose the close communication and fellowship that are vital to our spiritual health.

Luke 6:37 says, "Forgive, and ye shall be forgiven." Then in Matthew 6:14–15, we read, "For if ye forgive men their trespasses, your heavenly Father will also forgive you: but if ye forgive not men their trespasses, neither will your Father forgive your trespasses." Will God forgive us if we refuse to forgive others? According to this passage, He will not.

Hebrews 12:14–15 says, "Follow peace with all men, and holiness, without which no man shall see the Lord: looking diligently lest any man fail of the grace of God; lest any root of bitterness springing up trouble you, and thereby many be defiled." We must not allow resentment to linger in our hearts, for it will produce bitterness that will spread until it hurts not only us, but also others.

Let's remember the verse in Ephesians 4:32, "And be ye kind one to another, tenderhearted, forgiving one another, even as God for Christ's sake hath forgiven you." If we forgive, we will be forgiven. This is God's perfect way, and it is the only way to joy and peace.

Relationships

I clutched the shards of love that broke
On unkind words that anger spoke;
Relationship that once was great,
Destroyed by envy, lust, and hate.

Can anyone restore the old
When love discarded waxes cold?
"Forgive," says Jesus, "from within,
Forgive, and then forgive again."

When we forgive, we'll find there's room
For withered love to sprout and bloom,
For flames to spring from ashes cold,
And friendship turn from black to gold.

Plucked Flowers

One spring I planted flowers around our house. I enjoyed their beauty every time I stepped outside. I carefully weeded them, and soon they were blooming profusely. Then one day I noticed that on one side of the house all the blooms were gone. Curious, I circled the house, finding that every single blossom had been plucked.

I called the children to ask them about this, but they all claimed innocence. Then I noticed that our four-year-old was missing. As I sent someone to find him, I thought back to that morning when I had had to discipline him. Sure enough, when I asked him if he had picked the flowers, he replied that he had done it because he was mad at Mama. Harboring resentment against me for the discipline, he had gotten revenge by plucking every beautiful blossom. He knew how much I enjoyed them.

How often are we guilty of this kind of attitude? No, we might not pick someone's flowers, but our resentment shows up in other ways. For example, how do we react when, at the last minute, our husband changes the plans we have so carefully made? Or maybe we're asked to cut back on our grocery expenses, and then our husband spends money on something we consider unnecessary. Are we able to accept these circumstances with grace, or do we find ourselves fuming beneath the surface?

If we allow resentment to take root in our hearts, feeding it as we stew about things, it will grow into a monster. We may find ourselves ignoring our husband or withdrawing affection we usually give. We may think, "Well, he deserves it for what he did."

May we realize that bitter feelings of resentment, if allowed to fester, only bring unhappiness and broken relationships. This affects not only our relationship with the one whose actions we resent, but also our relationship with God. We cannot know peace with God when we hold resentment against another. We must ask God for forgiveness; we must also ask forgiveness of those whom we have wounded with our bitterness.

As believers in Christ, we are admonished in Colossians 3:8 to put off anger, wrath, malice, blasphemy, filthy talk, and lying. Resentment is borne out of anger, and is similar to malice when we act it out against someone. Those things belong to the old man. When we become new in Christ, we are to put off the old and put on the new. These new attributes are mercy, kindness, humbleness of mind, meekness, longsuffering, forbearance, forgiveness, and above all, love, letting the peace of God rule in our hearts (Colossians 3:12–15).

May we daily yield ourselves to Christ. As we allow Him to rule in our lives, we will find the power to live in a way that brings honor to Him. Let's not be guilty of plucking flowers to express our resentment.

I Go Apart

Sometimes I go apart and weep
For times that I have failed to keep

My Saviour first within my heart.
I know how I should live and act,

But oft' I let life's cares distract,
And cause God's blessing to depart.

It's then I go apart to weep,
And ask the Lord for grace to keep

My vision clear amid the strife,
For when my self is crucified,

I'll honor Christ who lives inside.
Lord, help me live a purer life.

Clear Vision

*F*or some time I had been having vision problems. Objects seemed fuzzy and lines appeared uneven. When the doctor examined my eyes, he found two cataracts that needed to be removed.

My impaired vision makes me think of our Scripture reading for today. With these cataracts in my eyes, I have trouble hanging a picture evenly. It is difficult to cut a straight line. My vision is not clear because it is obscured by cataracts. They need to be removed. That is the only remedy.

So it is when we have sin in our lives. We cannot effectively help others with their problems when we have a greater problem. Only when we ask Christ to forgive us and remove the "cataract" of sin can we reach out to our brother or sister.

We are warned in today's reading of the danger of judging another. Jesus tells us in verse 36 to be merciful even as our heavenly Father is merciful. Too often we are quick to speak against others and judge them. Jesus says, however, to mete out mercy, not judgment; to forgive and not condemn, that we may be treated in the same manner.

When our vision is impaired, we make wrong judgments. Our limited sight may cause us to stumble or misjudge distances. Only Christ can give us clear spiritual vision. His Holy Spirit will examine our "eyes" and reveal our need to us.

When Saul, a zealous Jew, persecuted the Christians, his vision was impaired. He thought he was doing right and serving God, but when Jesus appeared to him on the way to Damascus, God revealed to him that he had actually been fighting against God. Though Saul lost his physical sight for a while, he began to see spiritually for the first time. As Saul prayed, the Lord sent Ananias, a disciple of Christ, to him. Ananias laid hands on Saul, Saul's sight was restored, and he was baptized. From that time on, Saul's vision was clear, his focus on Christ. He became known as the Apostle Paul who suffered many things for his zeal for Christ and served as a shining example to other believers. (See Acts 9.)

Let's remember it is not our place to judge others. God is the One who tries the hearts. He sees what we do not; He knows the thoughts and intents of every heart. Nothing is hidden from Him. May we pray for clear vision and for love to forgive, to show mercy, and not to judge or condemn. Christ is the Judge of all. It is our responsibility to faithfully obey His commandments and love God with all our hearts.

Lord, Help Me See

Lord, help me see with vision clear,
To judge not, nor condemn,
Then mercy meted out, pressed down,
Will crown my soul again.

Lord, if you see within my eye
A splinter great or small,
Remove it quickly, so that I
Will stumble not, nor fall.

Lord, keep my vision clear and pure,
My focus stayed on you,
Till kind and loving deeds shine forth
And glory blazes through.

Freedom

*S*ometimes we hear people express dissatisfaction with their church or with the rules and restrictions their parents place on them. Their attitude is, "If I could just be free to dress like I want, talk like I want, go where I want, and be what I want, then I'd be happy."

Freedom, however, is not throwing off the restraints of church, parents, or other authorities. True freedom comes when we submit our wills to the Almighty God. When we insist on having our own way, we exalt ourselves. Christ wants us to humble ourselves before Him and others. Ephesians 5:21 says, ". . . submitting yourselves one to another in the fear of God."

When self is allowed to reign, we become enslaved in ways we never imagined. Satan uses every opportunity to bind us with his chains of pride, self-importance, and deceit, until we find ourselves in spiritual decline, perhaps embracing false doctrines that end in apostasy or immorality.

We need the church body. We need fellow believers who firmly stand for the truth, and who speak with us about our attitudes and faults. We need the Holy Scriptures and the Spirit of God. We are not qualified to choose our own way or to seek any freedom other than the freedom from sin that we find in Christ.

Submission to God is not always easy. Even Jesus had to submit His will to the Father's. In the garden He prayed three times, "Not my will, but thine, be done" (Luke 22:42). The Apostle Paul also realized that he had to submit his will to God when he asked God to remove the "thorn in his flesh," and God answered, "No" (2 Corinthians 12:7–9). God had called Paul to a great work, that of preaching the Gospel. Was it an easy road? No, Paul suffered many hardships—including being shipwrecked, stoned, and beaten—but he rejoiced, counting it all joy to suffer for the cause of Christ. Paul had found true freedom in Christ. The things of this world he counted as nothing. His vision was to win souls for Christ—to do the will of the Father.

This is where we find freedom—in submitting to God, allowing Him to do with us as He wills. When we have given Him all, we will thank Him for the boundaries He sets for us. Even though we may not understand the reason for all of them, we can accept that they are for our good.

Submitting to our husbands or other authorities can be difficult, but we will find joy in yielding our wills. Rather than straining for freedom, let's yearn after the righteousness that is from God. As we draw closer to Him, we will experience true freedom.

Finding Freedom

I longed to live without constraint,
To choose the way I'd go,
But did not see the path of self
Was fraught with pain and woe.

At last I yielded all my will
And Jesus set me free;
Then in my heart the conflict ceased,
For now I'm free indeed.

Guilty
by Association

is head in his hands, the young man contemplated the events that had brought him to this place—locked in a jail cell. He admitted to himself that it was the result of running with the wrong crowd. The previous night he had been with some boys who decided to break into a store and help themselves to the merchandise. This young man had protested, telling them he wanted no part in a robbery. They told him just to wait outside for them. However, when they entered the store, a silent alarm notified the police station, and soon the police arrived. They arrested this young man, assuming he was guilty because he had associated with lawbreaking companions. Now he sat wondering what the verdict would be. Thankfully, all the other young men testified that he was innocent in the matter. They declared he had had no part in planning or carrying out the robbery. He was released with the warning to choose his associates more carefully. As far as I know, he never again ended up in a similar situation.

Have we ever been guilty by association? When we find ourselves in a crowd of people who are using profane words against our Lord or are talking in an immoral way, do we stand up for the Lord, rebuking them for their words, or do we remain silent and hope they don't notice us? By our inaction, are we partakers of their sin?

In Jesus' prayer for His disciples and all believers in John 17, He did not pray for us to be taken out of the world, but that God would keep us from evil. He prayed that we would be one with Him and with the Father. As we experience the love of God, He will empower us to always stand for Him. He has called us to witness for Him. To win others to Christ, we must be willing to speak to the unlovely and sinful, not condoning their behavior, but bringing to them the good news of the Gospel. Jesus came for sinners. Let's remember that we, too, were sinners before we experienced His marvelous grace.

Bear Your Cross for Jesus

Will you bear your cross for Jesus?
Will you stand for truth and right?
Will you lose your life to save it?
Will you be God's salt and light?

People see the works we're doing,
Hear the words we speak each day.
How we live may then determine
If they'll choose the narrow way.

If we blush to honor Jesus,
If His name we fear to speak,
There will be at His appearing
No acceptance, though we seek.

Gladly bear your cross for Jesus;
Let this world be cast aside,
For we hold the greatest treasure:
Jesus Christ, the Crucified.

Growing in
Grace and Godliness

omen come in many sizes with various ages and nationalities. We are all so much alike, and yet so different. Each of us is a unique creation. God has given us different talents, abilities, and capabilities. Some have bubbly, outgoing personalities, while others have more serious, retiring natures. Some women find it easy to speak to strangers, but others struggle to find words to say. How boring it would be if we were all the same! God knew what He was doing when He made us as we are.

So should we just be content with who we are? Or should we try to improve when we can? Have we ever thought, "I wish I could sew like her; everything she sews is just perfect"? Well, what keeps us from asking her for some tips or some sewing lessons? Could it be pride? We may never know how much she could teach us if we do not humble ourselves to ask for her help. Humility is a virtue to cultivate.

Are we living up to our capabilities? One meaning of the word *capability* is "a talent or ability that has potential for development."[7] God expects us to use our talents to the best of our ability. That means growing! God does not want us to be content with mediocrity. Remember the servant who was given one talent and who hid it in the ground? Encased in dirt, it did no one any good, nor did it bring profit to the owner. God desires to see growth in us that will make us a blessing to others and bring glory to Him.

God has a plan and a purpose for each of us, and He expects the best from us. Each of us has a holy calling to follow God. Everything we do should have a kingdom emphasis. If our talent is cooking, singing, or whatever, we can use it to bless others. God gives us gifts to bless, encourage, and edify the body of Christ.

Ephesians 4:2–3 shows how the fruit of the Spirit promotes the growth of the body of Christ: "With all lowliness and meekness, with longsuffering, forbearing one another in love; endeavoring to keep the unity of the Spirit in the bond of peace." As we mature in our knowledge of Christ, finding completeness in Him, we will not be swayed like children by this or that doctrine, but will live in truth, growing up in all things into Christ who is the Head (see verse 15).

May we never be content to stop growing in godliness. 2 Peter 3:18 admonishes us, "But grow in grace, and in the knowledge of our Lord and Saviour Jesus Christ. To him be glory both now and for ever. Amen."

Whatever our personalities or talents, God wants to use us in His kingdom. He has a work for each of us to do. Let's keep growing in Christ and find contentment in the place He has for us in the body of Christ.

The Father Watches

Like a fragile plant that's tended
By loving hands each day,
So the heavenly Father cares for
The blooms in our bouquet.

Is my heart turned up to gather
His drops of love and grace?
Do I thank Him for His mercies
And thrive where I am placed?

Is my life for Jesus bearing
The fruit of joy and peace?
Are there shoots of faith and meekness,
And virtue's bright increase?

Father, help us to keep growing,
To learn of you each day,
To absorb your words of wisdom,
And fragrant blooms display.

Our Adornment

When Rebekah got her first glimpse of her bridegroom Isaac in the distance, she dismounted and covered herself with a veil (Genesis 24:65). This was a sign of submission to the man who would become her husband. In the first part of our reading today, Peter commands wives to be in subjection to their husbands. One reason for this was that if they had unbelieving husbands, their chaste and submissive lives might win them to faith in Christ.

Peter reminds us how, in the past, women of the Bible submitted to their husbands. He points to Sarah as an example. She called her husband Abraham "lord" (1 Peter 3:6). Peter tells us that we should not be preoccupied with the outward adorning of our bodies. He mentions the plaiting of the hair, a common practice among the lewd women of his day. He also spoke of wearing gold and fashionable or expensive clothing. Peter concludes that a meek and quiet spirit is supremely important. God values this very highly.

The word *meek* means "showing mildness or quietness of nature, and submissiveness."[8] *Quiet* means "not showy, grand, or pretentious; displaying calmness and self-control."[9] Our clothing reflects who we are. What assumptions might someone make based on how we dress or adorn ourselves? Whose fashions do we follow? Are we more concerned about adorning our bodies than we are about cultivating a meek and quiet spirit? The commentator Matthew Henry believed you could gauge the vanity of a person's mind by the brightness and gaudiness of her dress.[10] Perhaps we should ask, is what we wear a source of temptation for men? Does the pattern we choose, the tight or short skirts, the low necklines, or other adornment draw their eyes to us?

Timothy writes in 1 Timothy 2:9 that women should adorn themselves with modest apparel, not with a bold spirit, but with seriousness. Christian women are to put on more excellent ornaments, ornaments that are not corruptible (1 Peter 3:4). What we put on this body will perish, but by the grace of God, the ornament of a meek and quiet spirit will never lose its value.

As we seek to adorn the inner person, we will be less concerned about our outward appearance. May we ask God to reveal what is in our hearts, searching our motives and desires. Oh, that we would catch the vision of the godly women God wants us to be! We do not need to promote ourselves or our bodies as the world does, but, in obedience to the Scriptures, follow God with a meek and quiet spirit, the ornament of great price.

Jesus, I Would Learn of You

Jesus, I would learn of you,
Learn your manner meek and mild,
Daily seek to copy you,
Trust you as a little child.

Jesus, I would learn of you,
How you went apart to pray.
May I often come to you,
Read your Word, and then obey.

Jesus, I would learn of you,
Learn to love the way you love.
Daily may I seek anew
Streams of mercy from above.

Jesus, I would learn of you,
True compassion for all men;
When the lost I meet anew,
May I seek to bring them in.

Jesus, I would learn of you,
Learn to live as you did live
When your own tormented you,
When you prayed, "God, do forgive."

Jesus, I would learn of you,
From your fountain deeply drink,
Taste your waters sweet and true,
On your laws reflect and think.

Jesus, I would learn of you
Till your image I portray;
Let my heart be filled with you
Every hour of every day.

Scripture reading: Galatians 5:22–26

True Beauty

Years ago I knew a woman with a personality so pleasant and a smile so winsome that I hardly noticed that her face was quite homely. Her kind ways drew people to her, and her love for God shone in all she did.

She could have fretted about her looks, retreated from others, or felt inferior. Instead, she rejoiced in the God who made her, and allowed Him to mold her into His image. She worked as a secretary in a Bible college. One year they captioned her yearbook picture with, "The beauty of a smile." Her smile reached out to others and touched many lives.

Dwelling on the things we cannot change never does any good. Although we cannot change some things about ourselves, God's grace can change us to be like Him. We can become women of worth. We don't want to be remembered as the cranky old lady next door, or the self-centered young woman who acts like the world revolves around her. Let's pray with the psalmist: "And let the beauty of the LORD our God be upon us" (Psalm 90:17). God wants to give us an inner beauty, the beauty of holiness, so we can display Christ to everyone around us.

Physical beauty will fade and decay, despite some people's efforts to slow down the aging process. Aging is a natural process. Our bodies are preparing to leave this world. As Christian women, whatever our age, we should glow from within. This glow is the beauty of the Lord that comes from being in His presence and allowing His grace to abide within us.

Proverbs 31:30 says, "Favour is deceitful, and beauty is vain: but a woman that feareth the LORD, she shall be praised." Women who love the Lord will daily exhibit the fruit of the Spirit. Is our joy and love for Christ apparent? Can people tell by our words and actions that we really care about them? How do we want to be remembered—for beauty that will soon fade or for kind and loving ways? If we are not happy with who we are, we must ask God to change us from within. Then we will become women of true, lasting beauty.

True Beauty

True beauty's not in face or form,
For these will change with passing time.
One day we'll gaze into the glass,
And say, "Is that face really mine?"

But beauty sprung from deep within,
Is that which as the years pass by—
When Christ has cleansed the heart from sin—
Becomes more pleasing to the eye.

Happy Are Ye

*S*eated in a circle with my spiritual sisters, I blended my voice with theirs as we sang softly. One sister after another arose to wash the feet of the sister beside her. Sometimes there were tears, smiles, or hugs as we expressed our joy in being able to wash each other's feet.

To some, this may seem like a strange thing to do. What is behind the practice of feet washing? In our reading today, Jesus washed his disciples' feet on the night He was betrayed. Jesus said in verse 14, "If I then, your Lord and Master, have washed your feet; ye also ought to wash one another's feet."

Earlier when Jesus wanted to wash Peter's feet, Peter had protested. He did not want his Master to perform this act of servitude. Jesus, however, reproved him, saying, "If I wash thee not, thou hast no part with me" (John 13:8). Immediately Peter asked Jesus to wash his hands and head as well. Jesus assured Peter that it was enough to wash his feet.

The backdrop of this scene is Jesus' consciousness that the time had nearly come when He would leave this world and go to His Father. John 13:1 says, "Having loved his own which were in the world, he loved them unto the end." Was this act of washing His disciples' feet a way to demonstrate His love for them? As He taught them to be servants to one another, He also taught them humility. Then Christ said, "If ye know (or understand) these things, happy are ye, if ye do them" (John 13:17).

In my circle of sisters some were young, some old, some rich, and some poor. In Christ, however, we were on common ground, equal before the Lord. We were one in Christ, and as His love flowed through us, we were eager to wash each other's feet. This physical act serves as a tangible reminder of the way we ought to walk together in daily life. As we practice humble service by helping to meet each other's needs, sharing our joys and sorrows, forgiving, and encouraging, the act of feet washing becomes even more meaningful.

Jesus said that whatever we do in His name, it is as if we did it to Him. We can't literally wash the feet of Christ, but we can love our sister with His love. We can serve our sister in the name of Christ.

Consider the words of Philippians 2:5–8: "Let this mind be in you, which was also in Christ Jesus: who, being in the form of God, thought it not robbery to be equal with God: but made himself of no reputation, and took upon him the form of a servant, and was made in the likeness of men: and being found in fashion as a man, he humbled himself, and became obedient unto death, even the death of the cross."

When Jesus knelt before His disciples to wash their feet, He showed them how much He loved them. Even as He humbled Himself that night, He would soon humble Himself to die on the cross. May we count it all joy to serve with humility, even washing our sister's feet. Happy are the people who follow God in all things.

In True Humility

Jesus, finished with the meal,
Arose and left His seat,
And humbly knelt upon the floor,
To wash His servants' feet.

If you would example take,
Then wash your sisters' feet.
Serving others every day,
To Christ an offering sweet.

How can we refuse to bow
And wash our sisters' feet
When Jesus sprinkled His own blood
Upon the mercy seat?

Happy will that sister be
Who Jesus' Word obeys.
May our hearts desire to serve,
And follow in His ways.

Our Tongues: Good or Evil?

*H*ow often have we been wounded by someone's words? In Psalm 52:2–3, David speaks of those who lied about him: "Thy tongue deviseth mischief; like a sharp razor, working deceitfully. Thou lovest evil more than good; and lying rather than to speak righteousness." Psalm 57:4 likens the tongue to a sharp sword. Yes, words can pierce, especially when they come from someone close to us.

As wives and mothers, are we like the woman described in Proverbs 31:26? "She openeth her mouth with wisdom; and in her tongue is the law of kindness." Proverbs 12:18 speaks of words that are like the "piercings of a sword," but "the tongue of the wise is health." Proverbs 15:4 describes a wholesome tongue as "a tree of life." A good tongue speaks words that are healing, words that restore relationships. An evil tongue, however, only wounds and destroys.

Do we always speak the truth? Are we guilty of tale bearing or slander? Are we ever guilty of flattery? Proverbs 12:22 tells us what God thinks about this: "Lying lips are abomination to the LORD: but they that deal truly are his delight." Proverbs 26:28 adds, "A lying tongue hateth those that are afflicted by it; and a flattering mouth worketh ruin." Behind the lying tongue often lies the barb of hatred.

Peter tells us that if we love life and want to see good days, we must refrain our tongue from evil, and our lips from guile (1 Peter 3:10). David writes in Psalm 39:1, "I will take heed to my ways, that I sin not with my tongue: I will keep my mouth with a bridle, while the wicked is before me." Often it is in the heat of anger that we speak words we later regret. James 3:8 tells us that no man can tame the tongue. When we cry out to God, however, He gives us strength to control our mouths.

Job, in the midst of his afflictions, said, "All the while my breath is in me, and the spirit of God is in my nostrils; my lips shall not speak wickedness, nor my tongue utter deceit" (Job 27:3–4). His desire was to live a righteous life. David used his tongue to speak of God's righteousness, and to praise Him all the day long (Psalm 35:28). In Psalm 51:14, he declares, ". . . my tongue shall sing aloud of thy righteousness." If we fill our minds with the things of God, we will find it easier to use our tongues in ways that please Him.

1 John 3:18 says, "My little children, let us not love in word, neither in tongue; but in deed and in truth." The words we say are important. They should be kind, truthful words that do not tear down others, but rather build them up. Our words will leave a lasting impression on our children. Our children learn how to live and talk by observing the way we live and talk. Psalm 119:11 provides a good challenge for us: "Thy word have I hid in mine heart, that I might not sin against thee." The psalmist constantly sought to know more of God's law. He prayed that God would remove from him the way of lying (Psalm 119:29). May we also have a heart that yearns to know and obey God's Word. May the words of Proverbs 10:20 be true of us: "The tongue of the just is as choice silver."

The Tongue

The tongue is but a member small
That wields a power great
To utter words that cheer and heal,
Or spew forth words of hate.

In God alone we find the power
To use our tongues aright,
To shower words of kindness that
Bring hope in someone's night.

Remember, all our words are known,
From God we cannot hide;
Before we speak, He knows our thoughts.
O Lord, in us abide.

Speaking Slander

"Did you hear what they're saying about Martha's daughter? I can't believe she did that! Oh, and I heard someone say they're pretty sure it was the bishop's son that they saw smoking. I don't know who it was that saw him, but isn't that awful? To think the bishop's son would do that."

Haven't we all heard someone's character maligned? Are we eager to hear the details of these allegations? Do we add our own two cents' worth?

In Psalm 15:1, David questions God, "Who shall abide in thy tabernacle?" In today's words, we might ask, "God, who will make it into heaven?" In the rest of the chapter, David goes on to describe that person. In verse 2 it says he "speaketh the truth in his heart." A man who walks with God will want to deal truthfully and justly with everyone. The next verse speaks about not backbiting with one's tongue.

Taking a bite out of someone's back sounds rather crude, doesn't it? Slander always wounds. When we speak badly of someone, especially if we don't even know if it's true, we do irreversible damage. *Slander* is "a malicious, false, and injurious statement spoken about a person."[11] Proverbs 15:2 says, "The tongue of the wise useth knowledge aright." Even if we know something is true, we should use discretion. We should never use words to harm another.

Maybe we excuse ourselves because we said something without thinking. Proverbs 15:28 admonishes us: "The heart of the righteous studieth to answer: but the mouth of the wicked poureth out evil things." A righteous man knows that he must give account of his words, so he thinks before he blurts out words that he will regret later. We cannot recall our words, so we must consider how they will affect those who hear.

In Proverbs 25:28 we read, "He that hath no rule over his own spirit is like a city that is broken down, and without walls." If we have a problem with our tongues, we need to confess it and ask God to help us. If we have spoken unkind words to someone about someone else, we need to go to the person we spoke to, confess our wrongdoing, and ask forgiveness.

We should not be gullible, believing everything we hear. Proverbs 14:15 tells us, "The simple believeth every word: but the prudent man looketh well to his going." Do we consider what effect our words will have when we speak gossip or slander against another?

Backbiting is included in a long list of sins which are worthy of death (Romans 1:29–32). Those who slander take malicious pleasure in doing so (Romans 1:32). May we consider our words, being careful not to defame others. Slander may drive away the very ones who need the Word of Life. "Let the words of my mouth, and the meditation of my heart, be acceptable in thy sight, O LORD" (Psalm 19:14).

Keep My Tongue

Lord, keep my tongue from speaking words
That I will soon regret.
Upon my lips, O Lord, I pray
A guard you'd forge and set,

Lest I should speak a word and cause
Some little one to fall,
Or cause a wound that will not heal,
From dart I can't recall.

O may my tongue and all my thoughts
Bring comfort and reprieve;
Forbid that I should think or say
Some word that makes you grieve.

But may your praises ever flow
Out from this heart of mine
Until the words I speak aloud
Have been by love refined.

Making a Difference

How often do we wonder if we are making a difference in anyone's life? Maybe we think, "I'm just a housewife," or "I'm too old to do any good," or "I'm a teenager; what can I do?"

When we find ourselves asking these questions, we must remember that in God's eyes we are all special. He has a work for each of us to do. If we want to make a difference in someone's life, we must ask God to help us. We should make it a habit to pray every morning that God would use us for His glory.

One day I stopped in to visit an elderly lady. I meant to stay only a few minutes, but she was so lonely and eager to talk that I ended up staying much longer. Visiting the elderly is definitely a way we can make a difference. They often don't get out as much as other people. We can take them a small gift, offer to do errands or some cleaning, or just sit and visit. We will be blessed as much as they are.

We may never know the encouragement we have been to others. Sometimes it may not be the words we say, but simply our faithful walk with God which they observe. Perhaps they notice how we cope with trials or adversities. We never know who is watching us.

One summer shortly before our daughter's birth, the youth girls from church surprised me with fresh strawberries. They proceeded to clean and prepare them for freezing. That winter each time I served strawberries, I remembered the girls' kind deed, and appreciated their thoughtfulness.

We may not have the ability to speak before great crowds, or we may not have enough financial resources to significantly alleviate the needs of this suffering world, but God has a purpose for each of us. By giving a helping hand, listening to others, and showing our love and care in countless ways, we can make a difference in someone's life.

In today's reading, Dorcas had died, and the widows showed Peter the clothing she had made for them. Dorcas had made a difference in their lives, and they mourned her greatly. When Peter saw their grief, he raised Dorcas to life through the power of Jesus' name. This caused many to believe in Christ.

In 2 Kings 5, we read how a little maid's concern for her master Naaman made a difference in his life. Naaman was captain of the host of the king of Syria, but he was a leper. Doctors offered no hope for recovery. He had nowhere to turn for help.

His little maid, an Israelite captive, told her mistress that the prophet Elisha in Samaria could heal her master. When his wife told Naaman, he took hope and set out to find Elisha. Naaman was healed when he followed Elisha's instructions to wash seven times in the Jordan River. A little girl who spoke a few words out of kindness and concern made a huge difference in Naaman's life. May we, too, be faithful in whatever God gives us to do. We are called to love, obey, serve, and glorify our God. We can make a difference today!

Love Reached Out

Today I stooped to kiss a child,
And wipe away his tears.
I held him tightly in my arms,
And sought to calm his fears.

I met a friend whose face was lined
With cares too great to bear;
I gave to her a listening ear
To let her know I care.

I saw a beggar, poor, unkempt,
His visage marred by sin.
A smile, a prayer, a meal we shared,
He dared to hope again.

The child, the friend, the beggar man,
All three in urgent need,
So love reached out, and found a way
To do a kindly deed.

The Influence
of Godly Women

Throughout the Bible we find godly women who played important roles. Moses' mother bravely disregarded Pharaoh's decree to throw all male children into the river. She preserved her son's life for God's service. Queen Esther put her life in jeopardy for her people, the Jews. Eunice and Lois, the mother and grandmother of Timothy, faithfully taught Timothy the ways of God until he, too, became a believer. These women significantly impacted the lives of those around them.

I remember several godly women who influenced my life in significant ways. One was my pastor's wife who encouraged me as a young teen. I had just become a Christian, and although my parents attended church, they were not Christians at the time. Since there were only a few youth in the church, I felt alone. Her interest and friendship helped me to persevere in faith.

Sister Katie is another sister who really impacted my life. She ministered to street children in a small mission church. She was an older single sister who took us under her wing when we began attending that church. We were living away from our home community while my husband attended college. Sister Katie was a registered nurse who worked part-time at the same hospital where I worked. During the birth of our first child, she stayed at my side the whole time. Her comforting presence was like a mother's.

Later, when we moved to a new community, a sister in the church befriended me. She was like a loving older sister to me. She invited us to many of their family gatherings. She shared sewing skills with me. She even taught me to butcher chickens and hang wallpaper. One thing I learned from her was that to have friends, you must be a friend. The way she cared for her family and home inspired me. She was a gracious host, yet down-to-earth. Since we had no family nearby, she offered to care for our children during the birth of one of our children. Her thoughtful ways and godliness made a deep impression on me.

Godliness is a trait we all must cultivate. It does not come naturally; it is the result of spending time in the presence of God. The Word of God instructs us to show love and kindness to others. How easy it is to be selfish with our time, doing the things we want to do. I know these ladies who touched my life deeply had their own responsibilities to fulfill, yet they took time for me. What a gift!

When we display godliness, we show the face of Christ to others. Often our lives are the only Bible they will read. Are we willing to be His hands and feet? As women who belong to God, we are to be examples of godliness in our dress, our speech, and our daily life (1 Timothy 2:9–10). We are here only for a while, but what we do will leave an eternal imprint. 2 Peter 3:11 gives us the right perspective: "Seeing then that all these things shall be dissolved, what manner of persons ought ye to be in all holy conversation and godliness?" Let's allow God to use us for His glory. As we live to please Christ, we will become the godly influence on others that is needed in our world today.

What Do Folks See?

O Lord, help me, that folks can see
That I have been from sin set free.
My every word be pure and true,
And only that which honors you.

O may my daily conduct show
That you, O Lord, I truly know,
That I, through acts of purest love,
Direct their souls to you, above.

What in my life do they observe?
Which master do they think I serve?
Does what I do turn them away
Or point them to the narrow way?

O help me, Lord, to walk with you
In meekness, love, devotion true;
That I'll not lead some soul astray
By how I live my life each day.

The Perfect Quilt

The ladies sat around the quilt. Each woman's needle was busily making small, neat stitches—that is, all but one lady's. That lady held her needle awkwardly, unsure which position was best. Her stitches were uneven—some long, some short, some lopsided. Although she did her best, she had not learned sewing at her mother's knee. This was her first quilting bee.

One lady's eyebrows rose as she viewed the novice's stitches. A glance at her neighbor silently conveyed her criticism. Just then, the lady beside the newcomer gave her arm a pat of assurance. "Don't worry," she murmured. "Your stitches will hold well enough. Quilting will become easier with time. I am so glad you came today to help us." The tension eased as others, too, voiced their thankfulness for her presence.

A beautiful quilt is a work of art admired by all. The quilt produced that day was the product of many hands. Each one gave her best. For some, it was easy, no struggle; but for one, it was quite a feat. Sitting among mainly strangers, attempting an unfamiliar task with fingers that, unlike the others', were neither nimble nor fast, she felt the differences. But for that comforting pat on her arm and her neighbor's soothing words, she may never have attended a quilting again. She might never have experienced the joy of friendships begun in that circle.

In today's reading, Paul writes to the church at Rome, encouraging the Jewish Christians to accept the Gentile Christians. They were to bring them joy, to edify them, to strengthen them, and to build them up spiritually. They were to be likeminded with them and live in harmony with them. In verse 7, he tells them to receive one another as Christ had received them. The meaning of *receive* here is "to welcome and open your hearts toward someone."[12] Then together they could with one mind and one voice praise and glorify God.

As sisters, we have the opportunity to welcome new believers or those who join us to worship or quilt. How we respond to them may influence their response to the Gospel and the church. May we set aside our ideas of a perfect quilt or church and allow God's love to perfect us so we can reach out in love to those around us.

What is more important in the scheme of life: perfect stitches or perfect love? One will decay, but the other will endure. The Bible says in 1 Corinthians 13:8, "Charity (love) never faileth."

God's Quilt

Our lives display a pattern,
A quilt unseen by man,
With lights and darks appointed
By God's unerring hand.

We cannot see the stitches,
Or know when it will be
Completed by the Master
For all the world to see.

We give to Him our pieces,
The lovely and the plain,
And trust that He will fashion
A quilt to praise His name.

Sick or Strong?

No one enjoys being sick. Sickness robs us of strength and vitality. Sickness is caused by many things, sometimes a virus, an injury, the malfunctioning of an organ, or a cancer. Sickness hampers our ability to function as we should.

Sometimes in our spiritual lives we find ourselves growing weak. When we realize this, we need to seek help quickly. Perhaps we have failed to feed on God's Word or have neglected our prayer time.

Sin is another thing that makes us weak. When we disregard the dangers of sin, this sickness spreads like a cancer throughout our soul. The only remedy for sin is to cry out to Christ for forgiveness. 1 John 1:9 promises, "If we confess our sins, he is faithful and just to forgive us our sins, and to cleanse us from all unrighteousness."

When we are weak, we must confess this to Christ, asking Him to be our strength. Through His grace, we can be strong. We can say with Paul, "I can do all things through Christ which strengtheneth me" (Philippians 4:13). God wants to show Himself strong on our behalf. In 2 Corinthians 12:9, God told Paul, "My grace is sufficient for thee: for my strength is made perfect in weakness." When we rely on His grace and strength, not our own, He enables us to be faithful to Him even in tough times.

Psalm 31:24 encourages us, "Be of good courage, and he shall strengthen your heart, all ye that hope in the LORD." We must keep that hope alive and fresh. Our spiritual diet plays a part in this. What we read, what we think about, and how we spend our time will enhance or damage our spiritual health.

So when we feel weak and sickly, let's look to Christ. Isaiah 40:29 tells us that God gives power to the faint, and strength to the weak. None of us will make it to heaven on our own. We will never experience abundant life if we depend on our own strength. The Lord is our source of strength and life. When we stop depending on Him, we will soon find ourselves in trouble, for our strength will ebb away. Let's take time to wait on God in prayer, and He will give us strength to carry on and win the race. We can trade sickness for strength and be strong in the Lord.

> Be sick or strong, be right or wrong,
> The choice is yours to make.
> It's up to you; what will you do?
> Which highway will you take?
>
> The devil seeks your soul to claim
> Awake, dear soul, awake!
> Wash in that flow, be white as snow;
> Eternity's at stake.

Please Do Forgive

Lord, I've strayed from you today,
Sought for pleasures, lost my way,
Instead of kneeling down to pray;
Please do forgive.

Lord, I've failed to do my part
To lift some fainting, cheerless heart
When all her dreams were torn apart;
Please do forgive.

Lord, I've let my children down
As they gathered close around;
Could have smiled, but only frowned;
Please do forgive.

Lord, my actions I abhor,
And I need your grace restored.
Help me walk your way once more;
Please do forgive.

Lord, I know your Word is true;
What you say, you'll surely do.
Father, wash my soul anew:
You do forgive!

Sowing *and Reaping*

As a five-year-old, our youngest son greatly admired his older brother's motorcycle. He loved to be given motorcycle rides around the yard. However, we cautioned him that he must never try to mount the cycle on his own.

One day everyone was gone except my little son and me. He was playing outside when I heard him crying for help. I rushed out to find him pinned beneath the motorcycle. I quickly lifted the cycle off him. After I soothed his cries and examined him, he admitted that he had tried to get on the cycle. I asked him if he had forgotten the warning we had given. No, he remembered, but he thought he could do it without anyone finding out. He said he was sorry and would not do it again. Thankfully, he had only a few bruises on his foot.

Sometimes we are like my little son. We ignore the warnings given by God or by godly people. We decide we can do whatever we want to do. Then when things collapse and we are trapped, we cry to God for deliverance. The Lord graciously forgives us, lifting the burden of our sin. We may suffer more serious consequences, however, than the bruises my son bore from the motorcycle.

The law of sowing and reaping cannot be altered. Although we are forgiven, we still reap the consequences; we will harvest what we have sowed. Galatians 6:7 tells us, "Be not deceived; God is not mocked: for whatsoever a man soweth, that shall he also reap." May we learn early to obey God, seeking His will, so we will reap the good and not the bad.

What Is Our Life?

Life is but a fleeting moment in this space that we call time,
But the choices we are making show what's in your heart and mine.
God has sent His Holy Spirit to convict, to teach, to woo;
We must heed His tender pleadings when He tells us what to do.

If our sight were like the Father's, we would see how frail we are,
Would not yearn for things that vanish as the dew or shooting star.
For our souls shall live forever, whether with our Lord in peace
Or out in the darkness weeping where the fires shall never cease.

Jesus died for our salvation; through His blood He made the way,
If we let Him dwell within us, He will help us to obey.
Will you trust the loving Saviour, let Him guide your steps today?
What we sow will raise a harvest; for our sins we'll have to pay.

Spiced Peaches

We had tasted some spiced peaches at a friend's house, and liked them so well that I decided to can some too. They were a beautiful sight sitting on the canning shelf. One day I opened a jar, and my husband and I eagerly took our first bites. With a gasp of dismay, we laid down our forks and reached for our glasses of water. Our mouths felt numb. What was wrong? I remembered that the recipe called for a large amount of whole cloves. Although I had reduced the amount drastically, it was still too much. We could not eat any of those beautiful peaches. I threw them all away.

Some people are like those jars of peaches—beautiful on the outside, but full of sin and evil on the inside. Jesus compared the Pharisees to a cup that had been washed on the outside, but whose inside was still dirty (Matthew 23:25). Jesus told them that it was not what enters into a man that defiles him, but what flows out of his heart. He said, "For from within, out of the heart of men, proceed evil thoughts, adulteries, fornications, murders, thefts, covetousness, wickedness, deceit, lasciviousness, an evil eye, blasphemy, pride, foolishness: all these evil things come from within, and defile the man" (Mark 7:21–23).

David understood that God expects more from us than lip service. In Psalm 51:6 he writes, "Behold, thou desirest truth in the inward parts." In verse 7 he implores, "Purge me with hyssop, and I shall be clean: wash me, and I shall be whiter than snow." In verse 10, David prays, "Create in me a clean heart, O God; and renew a right spirit within me."

When we come to God with the "broken and contrite heart" spoken of in Psalm 51:17, God will hear us. He wants to give us a pure heart so it can bring forth fruit to glorify Him. The Pharisees' vain display of piety was repugnant to Christ, for He saw the evil in their hearts. We cannot hide our true selves from God. We must confess as David did, crying out to Him for a clean heart. Then we can serve Him in purity and truth. May we allow God to make us clean and beautiful within and without.

The Perfect Peach

The skin was picture perfect,
A lovely, luscious peach,
But when I cut it open,
It had a truth to teach.

For just beneath the surface
Of skin unstained and fair
Was rotten flesh and putrid,
Whose stench defiled the air.

Are there concealed within us,
Unseen and buried deep,
Some little "imperfections,"
Some sins we'd like to keep?

The blood of Christ is able
To reach those spots of sin,
Transform the base defilement,
And make us pure within.

The Cake

I stared at the box before me, crammed with recipes from the past. Most of them were spattered and wrinkled, their edges tattered. Selecting a couple from the box, I thought, *Some of these recipes have a story to tell. Red Devil's Food Cake . . . I remember that one.*

When I was ten, it was my favorite cake. Every time Mama made a cake, I begged for that one. One day she said, "If you want that cake so bad, you make it yourself. It's time you learned to bake."

I said, "Okay; I can do it all by myself."

"Are you sure?" Mama asked.

"Yes," I replied. "I don't need any help. I can read a recipe."

I mixed up the batter, poured it into the pan, and slid it into the oven. After half an hour, I took a peek. It didn't seem any nearer done than when I put it in. I decided to let it bake a little longer. Its chocolate aroma permeated the house.

"Is that cake about done?" Mama questioned.

"Not yet," I replied.

Finally, Mama came to take a look. If anything, the cake was thinner than when I had put it into the oven. Mama removed the cake, and said, "Now, Wilma, what all did you put into this batter? Why, I don't believe you even used any flour."

"Oh, yes, I did. I used that cake flour just like the recipe said."

"But we don't have any cake flour, just regular flour. What did you use instead?" she asked kindly.

"I used this," I said, holding up an empty box of confectioner's sugar. "I thought maybe this would work." My voice trembled. Mama smiled.

"It will be fine. Just let me stir some flour into this, and we'll let it bake again."

While the cake baked, Mama said quietly, "You could have asked for help, you know, if you didn't understand the recipe."

I nodded, "But I wanted to do it all on my own."

"Well, independence can be good," Mama said, "but pride is not. When pride takes over, watch out, because you're gonna fall."

"I'm sorry, Mama," I whispered.

She hugged me close, saying, "Let's check on that cake."

Soon my hungry brothers were asking to taste the cake. It really wasn't bad. I decided that Mama could fix almost anything. As I endured my brothers' teasing, I decided, "Next time I won't be too proud to ask for help if I need it."

God wants us to be humble. When we have a proud spirit, we allow self to have its way. Luke 14:11 says, "For whosoever exalteth himself shall be abased; and he that humbleth himself shall be exalted." Proverbs 16:18 reminds us, "Pride goeth before destruction, and an haughty spirit before a fall." 1 Peter 5:6 says, "Humble yourselves therefore under the mighty hand of God, that he may exalt you in due time." Let's remember that pride can produce much more disastrous results than a flopped cake.

Search Our Hearts

Those who have a haughty spirit,
Those with a conceited look,
Are disdained by God,
Chided in His Book.

Jesus wants us meek in spirit,
Walking in humility;
Children of the light;
Little christs are we.

Search our hearts, O God, and see
If there hides presumptuous sin.
Purify our hearts;
May you dwell within.

The Body of Christ

*S*ometimes when I sit in church, I am amazed by the thought that I am part of the body of Christ. As I glance at the other worshipers, I think, *We are one in Christ.* Listening to missionary speakers or reading mission newsletters enlarges my concept of the body of Christ. Around the world, believers are joined together as part of Jesus Christ's body. What a glorious thought!

Too often, though, we forget that we are but one of many. We believe the world revolves around us. We want our needs met, our hurts noticed, our desires granted. We act like the child who demands that things be done his way. If not, he pouts, "Then I won't play anymore."

Can't we see how this damages the body of Christ? Our self-centeredness does not promote growth; it causes the body to limp along, struggling to keep its balance.

While we demand our way, some become discouraged and fall away or withdraw from the body. Scripture instructs us to build up one another in the Lord (Jude 20). We need to genuinely care for each other and listen to our brothers' and sisters' concerns.

When things are not done to our satisfaction, do we become upset, nursing our anger or disappointment? If what is done does not violate Scripture, a good recourse is to lay it down and be at peace with our brother or sister.

Does God want to accomplish something in us through this experience? We can allow God to mold us, polish us, and shape us according to His design so we can enhance the body of Christ, or we can become a shriveled member who hinders the functions of the body.

What great things could be accomplished for the kingdom of God if the whole body of Christ would pull together as one! God gives strength and power to those who go forth in His name. We need to stand together against the evil one instead of bickering among ourselves.

Let's bind up one another's wounds, pouring on the oil of love and forgiveness, helping each other on the way to heaven. May our mentality not be "me," but "we," remembering we are all "His." May others be able to see our love for each other.

Jesus Prayed

Jesus prayed for His disciples
And for all who would believe,
Prayed that we would love each other,
So His blessing we'd receive.

Jesus prayed that God would guard us
In this world enslaved by sin,
Give us grace to love each other,
Then go bring the lost ones in.

Jesus died for every person,
Died to set us free from sin.
We can help our neighbors find Him
By reflecting Christ within.

But if someone's searching, longing
For the peace and joy we know,
They might fail to meet the Saviour
If we treat them as a foe.

When we serve each other kindly,
All the world will see our love.
But if we don't love each other,
How will they see God above?

True Worship

Have you ever watched children "playing church"? Children who have always been taken to church know just how to do it. They take turns singing, praying, and preaching. We smile at them, but I wonder, how often are we guilty of "playing church"?

1 Chronicles 16:29 commands: "Give unto the LORD the glory due unto his name: bring an offering, and come before him: worship the LORD in the beauty of holiness." Are we ready to worship the Lord if our hearts are not filled with His holiness? If we are not at peace with others, are we fit for worship? Jesus gives us the answer in Matthew 5:23–24: "Therefore if thou bring thy gift to the altar, and there rememberest that thy brother hath ought against thee; leave there thy gift before the altar, and go thy way; first be reconciled to thy brother, and then come and offer thy gift."

Because God is holy, He wants a holy people. Often God told His people, "Ye shall be holy: for I the LORD your God am holy" (Leviticus 19:2). In Isaiah 6:3, one of the seraphim cried, "Holy, holy, holy, is the LORD of hosts: the whole earth is full of his glory." Worship is not about us; worship is about the great God who made us, redeemed us, and will someday return for His own. As we focus on God and His holiness, true worship springs forth from our hearts. True worship changes our lives so we can truly bring glory to Him.

While speaking to the Pharisees and scribes, Jesus quoted the words of Isaiah: "As it is written, this people honoureth me with their lips, but their heart is far from me. Howbeit in vain do they worship me, teaching for doctrines the commandments of men" (Mark 7:6–7).

The words we say and the gifts we bring are abhorrent to God if our hearts are far from Him. God is the revealer of hearts. If we listen, He will show us what is in our hearts. Then we must humble ourselves and allow Him to cleanse us. Only then we can worship God in the beauty of holiness.

Psalm 96:6–9 describes what our attitude should be in worship: "Honour and majesty are before him: strength and beauty are in his sanctuary. Give unto the LORD, O ye kindreds of the people, give unto the LORD glory and strength. Give unto the LORD the glory due unto his name: bring an offering, and come into his courts. O worship the LORD in the beauty of holiness: fear before him, all the earth." What can we offer to God but ourselves?

Like the psalmist in Psalm 84:2, our hearts should long to worship God: "My soul longeth, yea, even fainteth for the courts of the LORD: my heart and my flesh crieth out for the living God."

When God is our life, we will desire to worship Him not just at church, but at home throughout the day, and even when we wake up at night. We have a great, magnificent God who has blessed us beyond measure. Let's worship Him in truth and the beauty of holiness.

Worship Christ

Behold the Lamb of Calvary
Whose blood our ransom bought.
Bow down and render to His name
Acclaim for what He's wrought.

Come now, and worship Christ our King—
Redeemed humanity—
He broke the chains that kept us slaves,
And bought our liberty.

Break forth in songs of highest praise,
His matchless power tell
Till all the world takes up the chant,
"He doeth all things well."

O let our praise ascend on high,
And may our hearts esteem
The Christ of God, our risen Lord,
For He our souls redeemed.

Behold His might and power displayed,
His grace and purity,
The brightness of His countenance,
Unmasked divinity.

Come now and worship Christ our Lord,
Let joyful praises ring.
All glory, honor, love is due
To Jesus Christ our King.

For God's Glory

I examined the crosscut saw on the table before me. It was coated with dust and grime from years of disuse. What concerned me, however, were the spots of rust I saw. I cleaned the saw as well as I could and then started my hand sander. I sanded the rust spots until the surface was clean and smooth. Then it was ready to be primed. After that I would paint a picture on its surface.

How like that saw we are, I thought. Living in this world of sin, we accumulate dust and grime. Our hearts become corroded with sin spots that we cannot remove. Eventually they will destroy our souls just as that saw, if left alone, would soon crumble with rust. Like the psalmist, we must cry out, "Help us, O God of our salvation, for the glory of thy name: and deliver us, and purge away our sins, for thy name's sake" (Psalm 79:9).

We need to yield to the Holy Spirit, allowing Him to show us our need for cleansing. Then, as we allow the abrasive power of God's Word and the blood of Jesus to remove all the sin spots, God makes us into vessels for His glory. Our testimony becomes that of Romans 6:22: "But now being made free from sin, and become servants to God, ye have your fruit unto holiness, and the end everlasting life." We are told in Ephesians 4:22–24 to put off the old life of sin and to put on the new man who is created in righteousness and true holiness. This is the life that brings glory to God.

When a painting or other work of art is viewed by others, it is not the work that receives acclaim or glory, but the artist. Even so, we should not receive glory for the work Christ has wrought in and through us; God should receive the glory.

An artist can choose to put any scene on the canvas. Likewise, God chooses the colors He will use to make us a work of His design. Sometimes bright colors or dark shades fill our lives, but it is God who receives the glory when the picture is completed.

In Isaiah 43:7, God declares His purpose in creating us: "I have created him for my glory, I have formed him; yea, I have made him." Isaiah 43:21 says, "This people have I formed for myself; they shall show forth my praise." Psalm 79:13 describes the response God desires: "So we thy people and sheep of thy pasture will give thanks for ever: we will shew forth thy praise to all generations." Often an artist's work becomes more valuable as the years go by, even after his death. If we praise God by the way we live, and we tell our children and grandchildren what the Lord has done for us, we will leave a legacy that will glorify God for years to come.

May we allow God to create His "picture" on our lives. On our own, we can never produce any beauty. Whatever good we may accomplish in this life is not to our credit, but God's. "He that glorieth, let him glory in the Lord" (1 Corinthians 1:31).

Give God Glory

How do we give God glory?
With reverent words alone?
Or is it by our actions,
By deeds of kindness sown?

The words expressed so kindly,
The hands reached out in love
Reflect the Saviour's presence,
And point to God above.

To God be all the glory;
To Him be all the praise.
With hearts and lips and actions,
Tribute to Him we raise.

A Faithful
Life

She was old, whitehaired, and wrinkled. She sat on a rocking chair on the long front porch. Although her hands lay motionless in her lap, her eyes followed the activity in the neighboring yard where children played. She could not see them clearly, for cataracts dimmed her vision. Though her hearing was no longer keen, she could still discern the children's peals of laughter. Their innocent fun brought a smile to her face.

Often these days her mind was not clear. She confused the names of children, grandchildren, and great-grandchildren. There were too many to keep them all straight. Sometimes she called for "Dad," her beloved husband of sixty years, who had already gone to be with the Lord.

At times she spoke of her childhood or the busy years of young motherhood. The old hymns and the name of Jesus brought a smile, brightening her face with joy. Often we heard her whisper, "The Lord is good."

Her family remembered her deeds of love and kindness, her faithfulness to God and the church. They recalled fondly the family gatherings at Grandma's house, sharing the good meals she cooked for them. They remembered, too, the confidences they had shared with her, knowing she prayed daily for each of them. Although in a way her days of usefulness seemed to be over, the godly impact of her life continued to bear fruit in the lives of her family and all those who knew her.

How do our lives measure up? When we face old age, dependent on others, will we be content with how we have lived? Will we rejoice, knowing we gave our best years to the Lord's service? Will our children be able to say we showed them the right way by our example?

When the psalmist wrote Psalm 71, he was an old, grey-headed man. His foes still stood strong against him. Even when we grow old and defenseless, Satan never lets up his attack on us. Like the psalmist, we must trust God to be our Rock and our Fortress (verse 3). In verse 5, he places his hope in God, even as he had done since his youth. In verses 9 and 18, he implores God, "Forsake me not." He rejoices in his God who has blessed him throughout his life and will keep him even when his strength fails in old age.

The psalmist's pursuit in life was to leave a testimony to generations to come of God's power and righteousness. By writing this psalm, he preserved these words for us to encourage us to live faithfully. Our lives pass swiftly. Soon we may sit still and helpless as the old woman. May we take to heart the admonition of 1 Thessalonians 2:12: "That ye would walk worthy of God, who hath called you unto his kingdom and glory." 1 Timothy 6:17–19 instructs us to trust only in God, not in transient riches, but instead to be rich in good works, storing up for ourselves a good foundation for the future, that we may receive eternal life.

Growing Older

My hair is turning whiter,
And my steps are getting slow,
But there is one thing certain
That I want the world to know:
In faith I'm growing stronger,
And the victory I can claim,
For Jesus' blood on Calvary
Has removed sin's awful stain.

Although my sight is going
And my strength is ebbing low,
I know I'll soon see Jesus,
And I'm longing there to go
Where I shall live immortal,
Evermore beside my God.
Don't grieve for me, my dear ones,
When I'm placed beneath the sod.

There's joy in growing older,
Knowing sooner I will be
Together with my Saviour;
Throughout all eternity
I'll sing the old, old story
With its message ever new,
I'll cast my crown before Him,
Give the praise that He is due.

I won't complain or worry,
Disbelieve or pine away,
But keep my eyes on Jesus,
For I know He'll make a way.
Why fret about the future
When God's hands are strong and sure?
I'm under His protection,
And His promises endure.

There's nothing can befall me
But the Father sees it all;
I know my God is with me,
For He sees the sparrow fall.
And God is fully able
To sustain me to the end,
Then take me home to heaven
All eternity to spend.

Part
THREE

Loving
Our Husbands

Scripture reading: 1 John 3:16–23

Love

Love is such a small word, yet its impact on others is potent and far-reaching. It links one heart to another, forming a chain that encircles the world. Its measure is unlimited, for its source is God Himself. Love is to be freely given, not hoarded. When we love unconditionally, we will see the effects of our love. Love changes others, and it changes us.

We often hear the expression, "God is love." Without God there would be no love, for God is the Author of love. When we reach out to God, we feel Him reaching down to us because He loves us. We realize the extent of God's love for us when we see how far He went to prove that love. John 3:16 confirms this: "For God so loved the world that he gave his only begotten Son, that whosoever believeth in him should not perish, but have everlasting life."

God placed within each of us a natural love for family, friends, and others. However, sin has corrupted mankind to such a degree that love is not always evident. Only when we belong to Christ and are filled with His divine love can we love as Christ loves. Jesus said it is easy to love those who love us, but the test is loving our enemies (Luke 6:32). In Luke 6:35, Jesus says, "But love ye your enemies, and do good, and lend, hoping for nothing again; and your reward shall be great, and ye shall be the children of the Highest: for he is kind unto the unthankful and to the evil."

Love is so important that the Apostle Paul devoted an entire chapter to the subject—1 Corinthians 13, the love chapter of the Bible. It shows the importance of true love, the kind of love that is only possible when Christ lives within us. We can do a lot of good deeds—such as giving all our possessions to feed the poor—but if our deeds are not done out of a heart of love, they are worthless. Even having great faith or sacrificing ourselves for others is worthless without love. We can prophesy, be knowledgeable of many things, including the Word of God, but without God's love within us, it is all to no avail.

1 Corinthians 13:4–9 tells us that love is longsuffering and kind; does not envy; does not boast; is not puffed up; does not act unseemly; is not selfish, but thinks of others; love is not easily provoked or angered; does not think evil of others; does not rejoice in iniquity; rejoices in the truth; bears all things, believes all things, hopes and endures all things; love never fails. How can we possibly love to such perfection? By loving the Author of Love. Jesus put it this way: "Thou shalt love the Lord thy God with all thy heart, and with all thy soul, and with all thy mind, and with all thy strength: this is the first commandment. And the second is like, namely this, thou shalt love thy neighbor as thyself. There is none other commandment greater than these" (Mark 12:29–31).

1 John 4:16 says, "God is love; and he that dwelleth in love dwelleth in God, and God in him." The secret of loving is just that—dwell in God. That happens when we confess that Jesus is the Son of God. Only as we have God in us can we love as He loves.

Let Us Adore Him

O how the Father loved us; He gave His Son to die.
What mercy and compassion—an infinite supply!
How can I help but love Him Who gave His Son for me,

Who pardoned my transgressions, secured my liberty?

O come, let us adore Him, and praise His name above
For giving us a Saviour, for showing us His love.
Our hearts and lives we offer; we would be His alone.
Someday we'll all be gathered around His great white throne.

O how the Father loves us and longs for us to be
A church that loves as He loves, that all the world may see
That we belong to Jesus, yes, we are one in Him.
So keep Christ's love light burning, and never let it dim.

Love
in Action

How often does your husband tell you he loves you? Every day? How often does he show you that he loves you? Both are important. On Valentine's Day my husband presented me with a bouquet of beautiful long-stemmed roses. He also gave me a card expressing his love for me. I enjoyed the roses and the card. However, I treasure even more the ways he expresses his love for me daily. He goes to work to provide for our needs. He does the vacuuming for me weekly, since I am unable to do it. He willingly takes me here and there, and he listens to me when I talk about my hobbies and interests. In countless ways, he shows that he cares for me.

How often do we tell God that we love Him? Every day? We should. I believe God enjoys hearing the words from our lips. How often do we show God that we love Him? Our actions show whether or not the words we say are true.

We know that God loves us because He sent His only Son to be the propitiation for our sins (1 John 4:10). 1 John 3:1 says, "Behold, what manner of love the Father hath bestowed upon us, that we should be called the sons of God." This is a great gift—to be sons and daughters of God, with all the privileges of being His children. He is the Source of all good gifts, as it says in James 1:17: "Every good gift and every perfect gift is from above, and cometh down from the Father of lights."

1 John 4:11 tells us, "Beloved, if God so loved us, we ought also to love one another." In verses 20–21, we see that we cannot hate our

brother and say that we love God. God commands that if we love Him, we must love our brother also.

The Apostle John wrote in 3 John 1:4, "I have no greater joy than to hear that my children walk in truth." 2 John 1:6 says, "And this is love, that we walk after his commandments." We show God our love by obeying His commandments, walking in truth, and keeping alive our faith in Christ. If we do these things, God will help us to overcome.

We want to someday be part of that group that will say, "Worthy is the Lamb that was slain to receive power, and riches, and wisdom, and strength, and honour, and glory, and blessing" (Revelation 5:12). Our love will find its fulfillment in perfect worship and praise of the Lamb who was slain, and the joy of being in His presence. Let's love in word and in deed, with all our heart, soul, strength, and mind. "Keep yourselves in the love of God, looking for the mercy of our Lord Jesus Christ unto eternal life" (Jude 21).

Love, a Word of Action

The test of love is action.
It has to be that way;
We can't belong to Jesus
And not His love display.

Love reaches out to others—
The hungry, sick, and poor;
When love helps bear their burdens,
It opens up the door

To tell them of the Saviour,
Their one eternal Friend,
Who came to earth from glory,
And loved them to the end.

So show the world the Saviour
By loving deeds you do.
With love, proclaim the message
That Jesus loves them too.

"Slick" Dumplings

Before I opened the door, the smell of chicken simmering was already tantalizing my taste buds. *Mama must be making creamed chicken or chicken and dumplings.* I stepped inside, closing the door. *Yes, it must be chicken and dumplings; I could tell by the smile on Daddy's face.*

Slipping into the kitchen, I gave Mama a hug. I stood watching as she gathered the ingredients, mixed, and rolled out the dumplings. She always rolled out her dumplings, which she made with only a little leavening, and cooked them in the broth. This produced dumplings with a "slick" texture. Once I asked Mama why she never made the kind of dumplings that were dropped into the broth by spoonfuls, like biscuits. She just smiled and said, "Your daddy likes this kind."

Mama was always fixing things my daddy liked. Nothing new there. "She must really love my dad," I thought. I can still see her standing there dropping dumplings into the bubbling broth and covering them to cook.

Whenever I smell chicken cooking, I remember Mama's love for my dad. Her actions showed that she reverenced her husband. She considered his wants and needs before her own. We children knew that Daddy's love for Mama was true and faithful too.

Love and mutual respect are needed in every marriage, but Ephesians 5:33 highlights one of the wife's duties in particular. The previous verses command a husband to love his wife, to provide for her, and to be the leader of the home. The wife is charged with the duty of reverencing her husband.

The word *reverence* means to "honor, respect, esteem, admire, defer to, adore."[13] Years ago, and in some settings today, a bow or curtsy expresses respect. How do we show our reverence for our husbands? One way my mother expressed her reverence was by cooking my dad's favorite foods.

Sometimes women demand equal rights. When a wife lovingly defers to her husband, however, she will find that her marriage is enhanced. Her husband will love her even more. How often do we praise our husbands for what they do for us? They willingly go to work every day to provide for us, and in many other ways make life easier for us.

A husband is to love his wife as Christ loved the church. We know Christ loved the church so much He died for her. When our love for Christ is what it should be, we will love and respect our husbands as we should. We might not make slick dumplings to show we reverence them, but we will find other ways to let them know that we hold them in high regard. Their opinions matter to us. Their counsel is important to us. If we would like more of our husband's attention, then perhaps we should give him more of ours.

Let's find ways to cultivate and deepen our relationships with our husbands. We can begin by reverencing them today. This is God's way. When we submit to God and to His Word, He will never disappoint us.

My Husband

My husband is so many things:
First of all, he is
My head or leader under Christ;
He is my best friend,
My encourager and supporter,
My provider,
My confidant,
My brother in Christ;
He is my partner,
My lover,

The father of our children;
He is a gift from the Lord.
All of these rolled into one make up
This special man that is
My husband.

His love and care for me inspires me to
A greater love and appreciation of him.
God wants us to be a team,
Walking and working together
In Christ in His order:
Christ, man, woman.

When we follow His plan,
We will find marriage a blessing,
And its commitment a joy.
Who is your husband to you?

Wise Women

Our reading for today shows us the importance of a solid foundation when building a house. This is true of our spiritual lives as well. If our faith is not built on the Rock, Christ Jesus, it will not withstand the storms of life, but will collapse like the house built on sand.

Proverbs 14:1 tells us, "Every wise woman buildeth her house: but the foolish plucketh it down with her hands." This house built by the wise woman may be a metaphor for her marriage. A marriage must have a good foundation. Both husband and wife need to have a relationship with Jesus Christ to provide that solid foundation for their marriage. What are some of the bricks a wise woman can use to build her house?

As I consulted some commentaries, I found the wise woman portrayed as a devoutly pious or religious woman. She is one who works diligently to care for her household so it will prosper. She manages well so their debts and bills can be paid. Thus, one brick could be good management. Mismanaged finances often cause conflict in a marriage. A wise woman will learn ways to live within the budget, respecting her husband's need to provide for his family and meet his financial obligations.

Another brick is faithfulness. We must never allow our affections to stray from our husband to another. Proverbs 31:11–12 says, "The heart of her husband doth safely trust in her, so that he shall have no need of spoil. She will do him good and not evil all the days of her life." If we feel we are not receiving the attention we need, we must not be tempted to look elsewhere for it. Instead, we must do our best to be cheerful, loving, and kind to our husbands. We should spend time in prayer finding God's strength to be the best wife we can be. We also need to be careful to keep the confidences of our husbands. He needs to know that his heart can safely trust in me.

The brick of respect is important. If I do not respect my husband, but undermine his authority, perhaps siding with the children instead of supporting his decisions, I have just removed a brick from our house. This attitude causes children to question their father's authority, making my husband feel defeated and useless. When I speak critically of my husband to others or put him down in the presence of others, it humiliates him, causing him to feel resentful toward me. I have pulled down another brick.

How can I build up my house? I must ask God to help me be a better wife. I need to surrender my will every day, so I can put others—especially my husband—first. I can show him I care by the little things I do, such as having meals on time, the laundry done, the house cleaned, and the children in order.

My son, a brick mason, enlightened me about mortar. This is an important ingredient in building a strong house. If the mortar is too thin, it will run all over and will not bond properly. If it is too thick, it sets up too hard, and may crumble. Love is the mortar of marriage, the bond that holds a marriage together. However, if I give in to selfishness, it is like the mortar that is too thin. The bond between my husband and me will become weak. Harshness in my voice or actions is like the mortar that crumbles. In contrast, loving and reverencing my husband strengthens the bond of our love.

Ephesians 5:33 exhorts the husband to love his wife as himself, and the wife to reverence her husband. As we put our husbands first, submitting to them as unto the Lord, we will be building up our house. May we not be foolish women who pull down our house by our words and actions. Let's be wise women and build strong marriages that will last. Although every day the divorce rate is rising, with Christ at the head of our home, and husband and wife in their places, submitting to and loving each other, our marriages will stand strong, enduring the test of time.

What Makes a Home

It's not a house of a grand design,
With furnishings both rich and fine,
It's not locale or landscaping,
Or artwork that is breathtaking.

But home is where there's warmth and cheer,
A place replete with family dear,
A haven warm and bright within,
Where peace is found 'mid kith and kin.

In homes by love and wisdom trained,
Where godly laws and kindness rein,
With people blessed by daily prayer—
We'll find true love abounding there.

Loving
Our Children

The Wonder
of Motherhood

I am going to be a mother! At first, I didn't want to tell anyone, I just treasured the knowledge to myself. I reveled in the joy I felt. The thought of one day holding a child in my arms was overwhelming. Praise to our great God welled up in my soul for showing such kindness to my husband and me. With that gratitude also rose prayers for the wellbeing of this tiny unborn child.

When I first held that little bundle of perfection, my joy knew no bounds. With the natural bias of parents, we were sure he was the most beautiful baby ever born. As we examined him from the thick black hair crowning his head, to the tips of his tiny toes, this verse in Psalm 139:14 came to mind, "I will praise thee; for I am fearfully and wonderfully made: marvellous are thy works; and that my soul knoweth right well."

I was humbled by this blessing of a child and honestly kind of scared. Would I be able to care for him properly? How daunting to realize that we, as parents, were also responsible for his spiritual wellbeing.

I am thankful that we are not alone in this endeavor. God and His Word are an unfailing source of strength and wisdom. Not long after our son's birth, we stood before our pastor and dedicated our son to the Lord, promising to raise him in the fear of God.

God blessed us with five more sons and a daughter. With the birth of each one, we again experienced the same wonder and awe. Each one was a special gift from God, and we thanked Him. I know we often failed, but God gave us courage to keep on trying to teach them to love and honor God. Even when the children are grown, a mother's heart yearns after them, wanting to see them follow God with all their hearts. They will never know all the tears we've shed or the prayers we have prayed on their behalf, but such is a parent's love. The wonder of motherhood never diminishes, nor does God's love for us. He is our heavenly Father who wants to bestow His good pleasure on us.

Jewels Rare

Remember when we used to wish for little ones to hold?
We longed for babies small and sweet within our arms to fold.
Their tiny forms a pure delight, their worth far more than gold.

And now, our lives are multiplied by sons and daughter fair!
We never dreamed we'd get to mold these jewels, fine and rare.
Our God in His great goodness has placed them in our care.

Help us, O Lord, as Mom and Dad, to teach these children right
That they may grow to be like you; they're precious in your sight;
And grant us grace and wisdom, Lord; we need your pow'r and might.

A Gift
from God

It was a stifling Sunday afternoon in August. The weather had been hot and humid for a while, and I was not handling the heat very well. The children were supposed to be resting, or at least very quiet, so their parents could get some rest too. I decided to check on our youngest, who was eighteen months old. Not finding him in his room or elsewhere in the house, I groaned, "Oh, no, I can just imagine where he is."

I headed outside. Sure enough, there he was playing in the sandbox with wild abandon. His blond head was already covered with fine white sand. I could have sat down and cried. This meant another bath and hair wash before church that evening.

As I gathered him into my arms, I realized he did not know the extra work he was causing. He was just being a little boy, enjoying the sand like all boys do. My thoughts went back to the first days of his life. He was born six weeks early, too tired to eat. I had to work hard to get a quarter ounce of formula into him every three hours. He just wanted to sleep.

Now I looked into his face as he smiled up at me. He had grown into a healthy, active child. I breathed a prayer of gratitude to God for the gift of this little one. Before I knew it, he would be past this stage of life, and I wouldn't have to deal with sand in his hair. Too soon childhood is over. Do we truly appreciate the gifts our children are?

Psalm 127:3 tells us that "Children are an heritage of the LORD:

and the fruit of the womb is his reward." The next two verses indicate that we should be happy to have many children, and not be ashamed of them. Like Jacob, we should think of our children as "the children which God hath graciously given thy servant" (Genesis 33:5).

We should treasure our children even more in this day in which we live. So many children are neglected, abused, aborted, or abandoned. How God's loving heart is grieved as He sees the plight of the children! May we be faithful mothers, loving and teaching our children by word and example. May our prayers also enfold the hurting children in the world.

Thank God

Thank God for toddling babies; we kiss away their hurts
And wash them nice and clean again from playing in the dirt.

Thank God for little children to brighten up our day;
They make a lot of work for which their smiles more than repay.

Thank God for all our children. What sunshine each one brings!
A home would be a quiet place without a child to sing.

Thank God for sons and daughters who cheer a mother's heart.
O Lord, we pray they'll never stray, nor from your way depart.

Communication

Five o'clock in the morning. I stood at the kitchen counter packing lunches for my husband and oldest son who would soon be leaving for work. Then I filled the lunch pails of our five school children. As I finished the task, I dropped a note into each pail and breathed a prayer for my loved ones who would be gone for the day.

That afternoon one of my younger sons gave me a note. It said something like this: "Dear Mom, Thanks for the note you put in my lunch pail. I like it when you write me a note. It makes me happy, and it really makes the day go better. So I hope you'll send me a note every day if you can. I'll see you after school, Mom. I love you."

That note brought tears to my eyes and joy to my heart. The communication between my son and me had blessed us both. I wonder if God feels the same way about us. He has written us letters of love and encouragement. Are we reading them? Are we communicating with Him through prayer to tell Him how much we appreciate them and love Him?

If not, let's start today. We will find that our days go much better, too, when we talk to our heavenly Father and read His letters. 2 Timothy 3:16–17 tells us, "All scripture is given by inspiration of God, and is profitable for doctrine, for reproof, for correction, for instruction in righteousness: that the man of God may be perfect, thoroughly furnished unto all good works."

We dare not lose the line of communication between us and God. Let's be sure to read His letters today, and be encouraged, strengthened, and instructed. How wonderful that God cares so much for us and declares His love to us in His letters, the Word of God! How marvelous, too, that we can respond to Him in prayer. God is so good. We should talk to Him often.

"My voice shalt thou hear in the morning, O LORD; in the morning will I direct my prayer unto thee, and will look up" (Psalm 5:3). "The LORD hath heard my supplication; the LORD will receive my prayer" (Psalm 6:9).

Love Letters

Lord, when I'm feeling lonely,
And perhaps a little blue,
I open up my Bible
For a tender note from you.

You tell me that you love me,
And you say that you'll be near;
Your words to me bring comfort,
And you calm my foolish fears.

You say that you are going
To prepare for me a place;
You say you're soon returning,
And I'll meet you face to face.

I thank you for these letters,
For to me they're treasures dear;
Within my heart I hold them
So I'll always know you're near.

My love I'll try to show you
By the things I say and do,
And when I pray, you'll know that
It's my tender note to you.

Despise Not
These Little Ones

*I*t was Easter morning, and I was excited. A few months earlier, at the age of fourteen, I had become a Christian. I had shared what had happened to me with my best friend and some of my classmates. Wanting my friend to experience the new birth, too, I asked her to come to church with me. Her family did not attend church. She asked permission to go, but her mother would not consent. Now, finally, she had said my friend could attend church with us. "What a perfect time to come," I thought, "on the day we celebrate Christ's resurrection." On the way home my friend told me she really enjoyed the Sunday school and church. She wanted to come again.

In the next few days, she asked me many questions about God, Jesus, the church, and my faith. She admitted she saw a change in my life, and she thought she would like to go to church again to learn more. That weekend, however, my friend informed me that her mother refused to allow her to attend church again. She said she did not want her daughter becoming a fanatic. Then she forbade us to be friends. I was unable to talk much with my friend after that.

A few years later, I learned that she was living with a young man, and had a baby out of wedlock. From what I heard, she had a difficult life, although she finally married the baby's father. How different her story might have been if her mother had allowed her daughter to learn of Christ and believe in Him.

Jesus spoke sharply to the Pharisees and scribes who did the same thing, "But woe unto you . . . for ye shut up the kingdom of heaven against men: for ye neither go in yourselves, neither suffer ye them that are entering to go in" (Matthew 23:13).

In Matthew 19:13–15, Jesus blessed and prayed for the children, laying His hands on them. The disciples rebuked those who brought the children to Jesus, but Jesus said, "Suffer the little children, and forbid them not, to come unto me: for of such is the kingdom of heaven" (Matthew 19:14).

Christ does not take lightly an offense toward a little child. In Matthew 18:6, He says, "But whoso shall offend one of these little ones which believe in me, it were better for him that a millstone were hanged about his neck, and that he were drowned in the depth of the sea."

As we relate to children or those young in the faith, we need to be careful to encourage them to follow Jesus. May they never see inconsistencies in our lives that would turn them away from the path of Christ. Like a small child watches his mother to learn how to do something, young Christians observe the lives of more mature Christians. What do they see? May we not be a stumbling block to them. We must pray daily for grace to live victoriously for Christ. Matthew 18:10 instructs us, "Take heed that ye despise not one of these little ones; for I say unto you, that in heaven their angels do always behold the face of my Father which is in heaven." May we never look down on any who believe in Christ, whatever their age, but humble ourselves before God, that we might not cause offense.

Faith Like a Child

Jesus says unto the children,
"Come to me, my little ones;
In my arms I'll safely keep you
Through the night when day is done."

Jesus loves the little children,
And they love the Saviour, too,
For their hearts are meek and tender,
What He says they want to do.

Give us faith like little children,
Simple, pure, unfeigned, and true,
So we'll come into your kingdom,
Your commands desire to do.

Like the children, Lord, we're coming,
Fully trusting you today;
For we know that you will hear us
When we bow our heads to pray.

Like the children we adore you
Your desire's our highest aim;
Take us, Lord, and ever use us
To bring glory to your name.

Follow
the Steps

Sewing was never my favorite job. I learned to do it mostly on my own, often through trial and error. By the time my daughter was old enough to learn, I hoped to make the way easier for her. First, I showed her how to lay out the material, how to place and pin the pattern pieces, and how to carefully cut the pieces. She thought these steps seemed difficult enough, and we were just getting started.

I explained that all she needed to do was follow the steps I showed her. I tried to encourage her that soon she would be wearing the new dress she had been wanting. Of course, things did not always go smoothly. When she sewed a seam unevenly or stitched the wrong pieces together, she had to rip out her stitches and redo it correctly.

Finally, the day came when she could sew a dress on her own. She had learned to follow the steps, one by one. She was thrilled with her new skills. I think she appreciated her new dress more, knowing all the work that went into it.

1 Peter 2:21 says, "For even hereunto were ye called: because Christ also suffered for us, leaving us an example, that ye should follow his steps."

As wives and mothers, and especially as Christian women, we have a grave responsibility. We have the opportunity in our homes to be a godly example to our children. They observe all we say and do. Are we walking with God as we should be, so they can follow in our steps? We are their living example of Christianity, just as Christ is ours. May we be careful to stay close to the Saviour, following in His steps.

Walk in Truth

While walking in God's truth, we find
A lighted path, and peace of mind.

For God extends His arm of grace
And guides us through life's darkest place.

Our love and faithfulness will show
When in His path our footsteps go;

And though the way be rough or steep,
Our Shepherd safely guides His sheep.

If we will do as Jesus taught,
And love each other as we ought,

We'll find Him near throughout the day
To help us walk the narrow way.

Then when we stand on Judgment Day,
We'll smile when we hear Jesus say,

"Now enter in, my faithful one;
You've made it home; your race is run."

God Doesn't
Forget

A coworker and I were chatting on our break. She was a single mother with several children. As we talked, she shared with me that at times she had been so poor that she could not afford formula for her baby. Instead, she fed him watered-down bean broth. Then she admitted that sometimes she had put beer into his bottle of formula so he would sleep longer, and so she could also rest. She told me she knew of others who did the same thing.

I was horrified that anyone would treat a baby this way. Expecting my first child, I could not imagine doing such things. Didn't she love her baby? Then I realized that though she seemed to care for her children, her desire to indulge herself took precedence over their needs. A goodly portion of her wages was spent on liquor and cigarettes. Food and clothing for her children took second place. Nights of partying were what she lived for. I tried to show her there is a better way, that Christ is the answer, but she shook her head saying, "I'm okay. Gotta have a little fun in life. Me go to church? Uh-uh!"

I have thought of her over the years, especially when I held my own newborn and tenderly cared for him. I thought of her children and their lack of proper nourishment, and the neglect and abuse they suffered. How thankful are we, I thought, for the training and love we received from our parents? But for the grace of God, I could have been born into a home like that. Although the government offers various programs today to provide food, necessities, and healthcare for children, their support is not enough. Without Christ, these mothers will never change. Their children will grow up to repeat what they have experienced.

In this age of abortion where the woman values her comfort over the life of her unborn child, we may think, "Doesn't God see or care about what is going on?" God does indeed see and care. Someday His judgment will be poured out on all who do such things. The little children belong to God. He does not forget them.

In Isaiah 49:15–16 we read, "Can a woman forget her sucking child, that she should not have compassion on the son of her womb? yea, they may forget, yet will I not forget thee. Behold, I have graven thee upon the palms of my hands; thy walls are continually before me."

Neither does God forget His church, His children. When the children of Israel saw their great city Jerusalem empty and her walls crumbling down, God promised to restore her and give her many sons and daughters. Through Christ, this promise is fulfilled as both Jews and Gentiles come into the kingdom. The latter part of Isaiah 49:26 shows us that God will triumph over evil: ". . . and all flesh shall know that I the LORD am thy Saviour and thy Redeemer, the mighty One of Jacob."

God sees everything and cares about us. He does not forget His own. Neither should we be complacent about the cries of the suffering children around us, whether they suffer physically or spiritually. God wants to use us to minister to the suffering and tell them of our God who cares for them. What are we doing to minister to their needs?

Let the Children Come to Me

"Let little children come to me," the Saviour said one day.
With open arms, He welcomed them; He'd not turn them away.

The Saviour held them in His arms, He blessed them as they came,
For Jesus loves the little ones who fondly lisp His name.

Across our nation every day, there are some who try to say
That taking lives before they're born is not a crime today,

But God determines right from wrong, and He does not agree;
He calls the little babies home, and holds them on His knee.

We hear about the great abuse to children all around,
Neglect, misuse, and broken homes; the tragedies abound.

When homes are shattered every day, who suffers more than they?
The little ones whose lives are crushed when parents move away.

In public schools it is a crime to read God's Word and pray,
Yet false religions are endorsed to lure our child away.

We need to guard the little ones, and show them Christ's the Way,
So they will know our God is real and pray to Him each day.

Our children are life's precious gems, we need to treasure them,
And teach them love for God above, then point them home to Him.

No matter what they're taught at school, they need the Lord today,
So help us stand for righteousness, and boldly lead the way.

Shutting Out
the Storm

One summer we sold our house and moved into a mobile home for a few months. As we settled in for the night, I surveyed all the boxes piled in the living room. I resolved to tackle them in the morning. However, with morning came a heavy thunderstorm. The children were distressed that they could not play outdoors. Their boredom and frustration made it difficult for me to get much done.

I stared out the window at the rain and the flashes of lightning, then closed the drapes, shutting out the storm as well as I could. I picked up the baby and gathered the rest of the children around me on the sofa. My oldest, always the responsible one, asked, "Mom, aren't you going to unpack more boxes?"

"Not right now," I said. "We are going to read one of the Little House books." My children smiled, and snuggled closer. I think story time was their favorite time of day. We read until lunchtime. By then the rain had stopped, and the baby had fallen asleep. The children ate lunch and went out to play. Finally, I could unpack those boxes.

Years later, one of the children recalled that day when we read while the rain poured down. He said, "With all those boxes stacked around us, it made me feel like I was in a tiny cabin. I'm glad you read to us that day, Mom."

I'm also glad I did. My children's wellbeing was more important than unpacking boxes. That time of togetherness is a memory to cherish.

That special time with my children, shut away from the storm, makes me think of how we can rest in our Saviour, shutting out the storms of life. In Him we can find peace and contentment. Our souls can trust in Him, just as my children found security in my presence. Psalm 61:3–4 says, "For thou hast been a shelter for me, and a strong tower from the enemy. I will abide in thy tabernacle for ever: I will trust in the covert of thy wings." Let Jesus be the shelter that shuts out the storm.

A Shelter

When storms of life are raging
And howling winds increase,
I have a place of refuge,
A place of perfect peace.

And so I rest in safety;
My shelter is secure;
Supported by my Saviour
Whose arms are strong and sure.

Teachers of
Good Things

In one way or another, we are all teachers. Titus 2:3–5 instructs the older women to teach the younger by their words and their godly example. They are to teach them to love their children and their husbands, living a life that honors Christ. The latter part of verse 3 says the older women are to be "teachers of good things."

This command applies to mothers as well. Our children's hearts are tender and pliable. We are called to teach them good and godly things. In today's world, many parents neglect to teach their children, allowing them to do whatever they wish. Sometimes children even tell their parents what to do.

Children learn by example. They watch our lives, copy our actions, and observe our responses to various situations. They sense if we love and respect our husbands even if they are not old enough to verbalize what they observe. Our children learn many things from us. Are we teaching them good things?

I remember going with my mother as she visited the widows on our street, usually taking them something she had baked. Sick neighbors also received a visit or a meal. Her kindness extended to the hobo who occasionally knocked on our back door. Mom always offered him a plate of food and a cup of coffee. She treated the hungry man with respect, and he thanked her graciously. I also watched my mother interact with the physically or mentally handicapped. Unconsciously, I learned that everyone deserves to be treated with kindness and respect.

Visitors to my childhood home never went away without sampling some of my mother's good cooking. Even when we had unexpected guests, she always found something to offer them. Hospitality was one of her gifts. When we stopped in for a visit after a brain tumor had left her unable to speak coherently, she would point at the stove and mumble. It was her way of telling us to fix ourselves something to eat.

Watching my mother lovingly prepare meals for my dad, get up early to make his breakfast, pack his lunch, and wait eagerly for his return home, taught me how to honor, respect, and love my future husband.

I also watched my mother cope with grief, and saw her experience a deeper walk with God. Her devotion to God encouraged me.

As we live, we are always teaching. We need to stay close to God to teach as He wants us to. Of course, we will not be perfect. At times we will fail. Then we need to ask our children to forgive us, but even that will teach them that we all need to humble ourselves and ask for forgiveness.

Be encouraged in the Lord. He will not fail to give us the grace and strength we need to be teachers of good things.

Help Us

These children, Lord, you've given us
To love and cherish, teach and train,
To lead them in the way of truth,
The way that you have preordained.

We need your help in this great task
Of raising them to honor you;
So grant us strength to follow through,
That they will want to follow too.

We pray for grace to sense their needs;
Like tender plants, they need our care.
In all their joys and trials too,
May we inspire with words and prayer.

And when we fail, help us, O Lord,
That we may not their trust betray.
We'll seek forgiveness at your feet.
To lead them in the narrow way.

You understand our hearts, O Lord.
We want for them life's very best;
But most of all, we pray that they
Will find sweet peace and perfect rest.

The Chickenpox
Siege

*I*n 1977, during the last week of school, our oldest son came down with chickenpox. One by one, the rest of the children succumbed to it. They were a sorry lot. Five suffering, uncomfortable, irritable children in our mobile home became quite taxing for us all. Because of all the sores on their heads, I could hardly comb their hair. The sores in their mouths and throats kept them from eating much. They consumed a lot of popsicles during this siege of sickness. Their father and I pitied them. We did what we could for them, but it just takes time to heal.

Time seemed to drag slowly as I cared for the sick children. As soon as one began to mend, another became worse. For six long weeks, I never left the house. The children were growing bored, too. One day some of their friends came with their dad. They stood outside, several feet from the house, while our children crowded in front of the window. How they enjoyed visiting with each other! Vacation Bible School had come and gone, with only a few of our children able to go. This would have been the first year for one of our sons to attend, and he was disappointed. We felt sorry for our children.

Psalm 103:13 says, "Like as a father pitieth his children, so the LORD pitieth them that fear him." The Lord looks at us, and pities us just as we do our children. He knows we are human and sometimes get into pathetic circumstances, but Psalm 103:17–18 says, "But the mercy of the LORD is from everlasting to everlasting upon them that fear him, and his righteousness unto children's children; to such as keep his covenant, and to those that remember his commandments to do them."

But we don't have to stay in that hurting, pitiful condition. Our heavenly Father cares about us and, unlike human parents who can't heal their children's chickenpox, God can change us. He can alleviate the pain caused by our sin. God promises in Psalm 103:12, "As far as the east is from the west, so far hath he removed our transgressions from us."

May we cry out to God as the psalmist does in Psalm 79:9: "Help us, O God of our salvation, for the glory of thy name: and deliver us, and purge away our sins, for thy name's sake." 1 John 1:9 promises, "If we confess our sins, he is faithful and just to forgive us our sins, and to cleanse us from all unrighteousness." How wonderful that our Father God pities us and wants to help us, just as we long to help our children. We can call on Him. Help is only a prayer away.

For Mothers

When the day drags along,
And the weather is wrong,

You are hurried and hot,
And you're flustered a lot,

Take a moment to pray;
It will brighten your day,

Give you courage and grace
To submit to your place.

When the baby's upset,
And he cries and he frets;

When the supper is late,
You just broke your best plate,

When your eyes fill with tears,
There is Someone who hears;

So just whisper a prayer,
And you'll know He is there.

In the
Night Watches

Many were the nights I spent in a rocking chair trying to soothe a sick or fussy child. While the rest of the household slept, my child and I were ensconced in a blanket in a world of our own. As I softly hummed the old hymns, the melodies comforted both of us. Those times, the night watches, became times of meditation and prayer for me.

Now that I am a great-grandmother, it isn't fussy babies who keep me up; it is pain or insomnia. I still find these are times for drawing near to God. As I read the Bible or pray, I am strengthened by sitting at the feet of Jesus.

What wife or mother doesn't have busy days? Sometimes it is difficult to find time for devotions when the baby wakes up crying and you need to fix breakfast, pack lunches, and get children off to school. For ten years I worked at our church school where our children attended. Mornings needed to follow a schedule, although that didn't always happen. I tried to have my devotions before I called the children for breakfast and then have devotions with them before we left for school.

Sometimes we need the quietness of the night to draw close to God. After the busyness of the day, those times with God are refreshing. Just as we want to comfort our child, God wants to comfort us and satisfy our hungry souls. As we reflect on all God has done for us, how He has been our help, we realize that we can rest in the shadow of His wings and rejoice.

The next time we are holding a child in the night hours, or just can't sleep, let's remember not to fret. Instead, we can relax, and let the presence of our mighty God soothe our souls. When we rest under His wings, we will find peace.

In the Night

In the dark of night I sit
Burdened by adversity.
But, though cares keep me awake,
I know Jesus sits with me.

And I find communion sweet,
As I read His Word and pray;
Then the cares that press so hard
Dissipate and fade away.

Then a song escapes my lips,
As encouragement I find,
And my heart resounds with praise
To my Maker, good and kind.

Whose Servant *Are You?*

How often do we, as mothers, feel like servants? Probably every mother has had those days when it seems all she does is cook, clean, wash dishes, do laundry, shop, and drive children here or there. Someone once calculated what a homemaker's worth would be if she were paid an average wage for all the duties she performed. The amount was astounding.

Some days we feel like we're nothing but servants. Then one of the children brings us a drink of water, "Because you're tired, Mommy." Another one offers a homemade card with the words, "To the World's Best Mom," and we're tempted to believe them.

Being a servant is easier when we realize that Jesus, the Son of God, became a servant. Philippians 2:7–8 speaks of Jesus, who "made himself of no reputation, and took upon him the form of a servant, and was made in the likeness of men: and being found in fashion as a man, he humbled himself, and became obedient unto death, even the death of the cross."

Jesus never said His servants would have an easy life. In John 15:20, Jesus reminds His disciples that even as He had been persecuted, they also would be persecuted. God called Jacob, Moses, and Daniel His servants. James, Peter, Paul, and Jude called themselves servants of Jesus Christ. So if we think we are merely servants, we are in good company. It does help our perspective if we realize that, first of all, we are to be servants of Jesus. As mothers, we get tired, but it should still be a joy to serve our families. We have so many opportunities to teach our children about God, and one is how we live before them.

Jesus said in Luke 16:13 that no man can serve two masters. Our devotion cannot be divided. If we struggle to accept the place God has given us to serve, we need to examine our hearts. Do we want to please ourselves, or do we want to please Jesus? When we are only concerned about ourselves, we are driven by pride and selfishness. We know that is not pleasing to God, so we must confess it as sin. Then Christ can reign supreme in our lives.

Jesus taught in Matthew 25:34–40 that the way we treat others is how we treat Jesus. He spoke about when He will return to judge the nations. To those on His right side, He will say, "Come, ye blessed of my Father, inherit the kingdom prepared for you from the foundation of the world: for I was an hungred, and ye gave me meat: I was thirsty, and ye gave me drink: I was a stranger, and ye took me in: naked, and ye clothed me: I was sick, and ye visited me: I was in prison, and ye came unto me" (Matthew 25:34–36). The righteous did not understand. When had they seen Christ in these circumstances? Then Jesus answered, "Inasmuch as ye have done it unto one of the least of these my brethren, ye have done it unto me" (Matthew 25:40). Do we rejoice that we are privileged not only to serve our families, but also our Master and Lord, Jesus Christ?

A Servant's Heart

O Lord, grant me a servant's heart,
The kind that wants to please,
That gladly seeks to do your will,
Instead of my own ease.

A servant's heart that will not ask,
"What will you do for me?"
But rather does the things you love,
With joy, wholeheartedly.

In that way I would show to you
The love I feel within
Because you loved me, Lord, enough
To die for all my sin.

Mothers, Pray

Mothers seem to have a basic instinct to heal the hurts of their children. From infancy, our children have looked to us to bind up their wounds, soothe them, and comfort them. Sometimes when they were small, all it took was a kiss, a hug, or a look at their "ouchie" and all was well.

As our children grow older, they don't need this kind of care as often. They begin to assume responsibility for their own needs. When they reach adolescence, we often hurt with them as they struggle with "growing pains." We long to fix their problems, to make things easier, and to bear their pain for them.

Even when our children attain adulthood and marry or step out on their own, our concern does not lessen. Through each adjustment they make, every crossroad they face, we long to help them. Often we must rein in our inclination to interfere or give unsolicited advice. There are times when our only recourse is to pray for them.

Prayer is the most potent "medicine" we can employ. Who can measure the impact of a mother's prayers? As we go about our work throughout the day, we can appeal to God for each child's need. We must spend time and effort for our children's spiritual wellbeing. Our prayers and tears will not go unheeded by our heavenly Father.

As parents, we are responsible to teach our children God's Word and way. Then, when we have taught our children the way to Christ, we must learn to trust them to the Father's care. Many sons and daughters have testified that it was their mother's prayers that kept them from taking the downward road.

We cannot force our children to make the right choices in life; it is up to them to choose life in Christ, or death. But we must not stop praying! It is our holy calling. Through prayer we can ask God, the Great Healer, to care for our children. He can meet their needs where we fail.

"The effectual fervent prayer of a righteous man availeth much" (James 5:16).

Pray without ceasing, the Bible says,
Later may be too late.
Souls are in danger, tomorrow's unsure;
Now is the time; don't wait!

Send your petitions to God above,
Send them throughout the day.
Never grow weary nor hesitate;
Now is the time to pray.

Your Mother's Prayer

Before your birth, I breathed a prayer
That God would keep you in His care,

And when within my arms you lay,
I asked for grace to guide the way.

The years have flown since that blest time;
Now you are grown, no longer mine

To take in hand and gently lead,
And care for every daily need.

Yet still my heart yearns over you,
My prayers still fly like arrows true

To Him who now looks over you,
Yes, even more than Mom can do.

What do I pray? That you would gain
Abundant wealth, exalted fame?

No, my desire is that you'd be
Washed in the blood of Calvary,

And that your feet would never leave
The narrow path, nor come to grieve

The cross of Christ, that spotless Lamb,
But cling to Him, the great I AM.

For when your life comes to an end,
Eternity then will just begin.

And what then would your treasure mean,
If you could not with Jesus be?

I want us all in heaven to be,
To sing with the saints, and Jesus to see;

Be faithful, child, stay by His side,
This is my prayer, your mother's cry.

Letting Go

I watched from the porch as my seven-year-old son strode down the walk to the front gate to wait for the school bus. He had given me a hug and had said, "Mom, I can wait by myself." As the bus pulled up, he waved, a big smile on his face. He was eager to experience his first day of school.

Letting go is not easy, especially for mothers. On the one hand we want our children to be independent, but on the other, we want to keep them near so we know they are safe. Throughout our child's life, there are many times that we have to let go and allow them space to grow and mature.

In our Scripture reading today, we see Hannah, a woman suffering the bitter pain of barrenness. One day as she and her family were at the temple, Hannah made a petition to the Lord. She asked for a son, promising she would give him back to the Lord to serve Him all his days. The Lord saw her earnestness and granted her petition. Nine months later, Hannah bore a son, naming him Samuel.

When Samuel was weaned, Hannah and her husband Elkanah took an offering and went up to the temple. There they offered a bullock and brought their child to the priest, Eli. Hannah reminded Eli that she was the woman he had observed praying. She said, "For this child I prayed; and the LORD hath given me my petition which I asked of him: therefore also I have lent him to the LORD; as long as he liveth he shall be lent to the LORD" (1 Samuel 1:27–28).

Although we don't know Samuel's age when Hannah entrusted him to Eli, I'm sure he was a younger child than we would like to relinquish.

It must have been difficult for Hannah to let go, but she kept her vow to God. Once a year she made a trip to see Samuel and to give him some new clothes she had made. I'm sure she made them with all the love of her heart.

We, too, should give our children to God at birth or before. We must recognize that they belong first to God. As we raise our children with loving care, we try to instill in them the importance of giving their hearts to Christ, loving Him, and serving Him. Daily giving them over to God helps us to relinquish our hold on our children.

When that infant is placed in our arms, we think we have a long time to prepare him for life on his own, but time swiftly passes. It isn't easy letting go, but when we release our children to the care of our heavenly Father, we know they are in good hands.

Let Go

"Let go, my child," God whispered,
"Let go, and trust in me."
But foolishly I clung to
My insecurity.

I had to learn the lesson
That God alone knows best.
It's better far to trust Him
Than struggle and protest.

Now when I hear God whisper,
"Let go; give all to me,"
I all to Him relinquish;
His will is best for me.

*P*art
FIVE

Grace
in Trials

A Refuge

When he offered this prayer to God, David was a wanted man hiding in a cave. Overwhelmed, he poured out his heart to God. His enemy had laid snares to catch him. David knew no earthly help. In faith, however, he cried out to the Lord: "Thou art my refuge and my portion in the land of the living" (Psalm 142:5). David prayed for deliverance. Even though he knew his persecutors were stronger than he was, he believed that his God was almighty. David chose to trust God and praise Him for His deliverance.

Sometimes we feel like we are holed up in a cave and that our situation is hopeless. Or maybe we think our troubles are too insignificant for God to notice or that they're too big for Him to handle. Impossible! What did David proclaim to the Lord? He said, "Thou art my refuge and my portion." David was placing his life, his hope, and his trust in God Almighty. He expected God to deliver him.

The first step to our deliverance is saying, "Lord, I want to be yours. You are the only One who can help me. I can't trust anyone else to fix my problems." Sometimes people look to their friends, their spouses, their children, or even their jobs for security and happiness, but our joy and peace rest solely on Jesus Christ. He alone is our deliverer. When we come to Him and surrender ourselves totally to Him, He becomes all we need.

Christ wants to be our refuge. He will give us power to overcome the assaults of Satan. When we face troubles and trials, only Christ can make us victorious. We need not lie down in despair or hide in a cave. Jesus longs to deliver us. He longs to show Himself strong on our behalf. God will not forsake us. He will hear our cry for help, and He will answer. If we cry out to God as David did and claim Christ as our portion and refuge, He will meet our every need.

David promised God that when He would bring him out of prison, he would praise His name. David believed that God would deal bountifully with him, and instead of being surrounded by persecutors, he would be compassed by the righteous. We must believe in God as David did, and then we can experience the wonder of joy and deliverance that comes when Christ is our portion. Then we will praise our mighty God!

Jesus

A strong and mighty tower, our hope in time of need,
His name is clothed with power, most glorious indeed.

Exalted high above all passing things below,
Instilling calm assurance wherever His blessings flow,

The champion of our future, when to His charge we yield;
We're guaranteed the victory when Jesus is our shield.

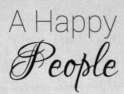

A Happy *People*

"Happy is that people, whose God is the LORD" (Psalm 144:15). When our children were small we would sing the song, "We're a Happy People." God's people should be the happiest people on earth. We have every reason to rejoice, for we belong to the King of kings. All creation is His, and the whole universe is under His control.

Yes, we face troubles just as others do, but we have Someone to help us through them. Jesus wants us to be a testimony to everyone around us of the joy He gives. How can we do that if we're down in the dumps? The closer we walk with God, the more we will resemble Him, the better we will know Him, and the more we will display His glory.

As wives and mothers we especially need to be joyful, for the attitudes we exhibit will set the tone for those of our family. If we're grumpy, others in the home will be grumpy too. A smiling, cheerful mother encourages her children to respond in like manner. To have a happy home, we must do our part. Staying in right relationship with Christ is the first step to being a joyful person and having a happy home. When we spend time with God and count our blessings, a song will spring from our heart and a smile will light our face.

Whether we are out and about or at home, we should let the love of Jesus bring a smile to our lips. If we remember to whom we belong, we won't be able to stop smiling. Psalm 9:1–2 says, "I will praise thee, O LORD, with my whole heart; I will shew forth all thy marvelous works. I will be glad and rejoice in thee: I will sing praise to thy name, O thou most High." Let's tell the whole world that we love Jesus and keep smiling.

A Candle

Father, help me be a candle
Shining bright for you each day;
Teach me how to be more loving
In the things I do and say.

Father, I would mirror Jesus,
Like a beacon in the night;
Let my life be like a candle,
Glowing softly with His light.

Father, let my light beam brightly,
Let it burn with holy flame,
So that those who view its brilliance
Want to glorify your name.

And Again I Say, *Rejoice*

Some of the recurring words in the book of Philippians are *joy* and *rejoice*. Within the four chapters of this book, these words are used fourteen times.

In the first chapter, Paul expresses his joy in praying for the Philippians. He joyfully brought his requests for them to the Lord. Is the church of Jesus Christ so dear to us that we experience joy when we think about and pray for each other?

When Paul wrote Philippians, he was in prison. Still, he rejoiced that even in his bonds he was able to preach Christ. His concern was not for himself or his own comfort. He had learned to be content in whatever condition he found himself. His concern was that the church at Philippi would stand fast and be willing not only to believe on Christ, but also to suffer for Him. Do we count it a joy to suffer loss for Christ, to give ourselves for the church and for the lost? Are we, like Paul, encouraging each other to rejoice in the Lord?

Paul had suffered much for the church, but he still rejoiced. In Philippians 2:15–16, he tells the Philippians that they ". . . shine as lights in the world; holding forth the word of life." Thus, Paul rejoiced that his work on their behalf had not been in vain. He was willing to sacrifice his life for them.

Paul reminds them in Philippians 3:7 that we have nothing to rejoice in except Jesus Christ. The Philippians could not trust in their heritage, their circumcision, or their own righteousness. Neither can we. We must remember that our only hope is in Jesus, not in who we are or what we can do.

Paul always demonstrated a joyful, thankful spirit. When the church at Philippi sent a gift to him to meet his physical needs, Paul says the gift was "an odour of a sweet smell, a sacrifice acceptable, well pleasing to God" (Philippians 4:18). Paul viewed their gift as evidence of the fruit in their lives. This brought joy to Paul. He calls the Philippians his "joy and crown" in Philippians 4:1. In verse 4, he admonishes them, "Rejoice in the Lord alway: and again I say, Rejoice."

If we obey Paul's injunction in Philippians 4:8 and think on what is true, honest, just, pure, lovely, and of good report, we will have much reason to rejoice. When our heart is fixed on Christ, what else can our response be but to rejoice? As we rejoice and encourage others to also do so, it draws us together, increasing our love and appreciation for one another.

In His Sermon on the Mount, Jesus spoke about rejoicing. His instruction to His followers when they were persecuted was, "Rejoice, and be exceeding glad: for great is your reward in heaven: for so persecuted they the prophets which were before you" (Matthew 5:12). No matter what our circumstances in life, we ought to rejoice. May we be faithful, dear sisters, to rejoice—and again I say, rejoice!

There's a Song

There's a song within my heart,
Such a glorious melody,
Praising God for all He's done,
And the joy He's given me.

For His love is tender, kind,
And His fellowship divine;
I'm so happy in the Lord;
I am His and He is mine.

So I'll praise Him every day
With a smile upon my face,
Thanking Him for blessing me
With His mercy and His grace.

I must tell the troubled world
How much Jesus means to me,
Precious Saviour, Lord of Life,
King of Immortality!

Be Joyful

or some people, joy seems elusive. They always hope to find it around the next bend in life with a job change, a different partner, or a new set of circumstances. It should not be so for the Christian. What or who is our source of joy? Speaking to the woman at the well, Jesus said, "But whosoever drinketh of the water that I shall give him shall never thirst; but the water that I shall give him shall be in him a well of water springing up into everlasting life" (John 4:14).

In Isaiah 12:2–3, we read, "Behold, God is my salvation; I will trust, and not be afraid: for the LORD JEHOVAH is my strength and my song; he also is become my salvation. Therefore with joy shall ye draw water out of the wells of salvation." Jesus Christ has made this salvation available to us.

In John 15:11 Jesus says, "These things have I spoken unto you, that my joy might remain in you, and that your joy might be full." Jesus wants to give us joy the world can't comprehend. When we belong to Christ, we have the joy of the Lord within us. This is part of our witness for Christ. The salesman who shows no enthusiasm for his product is certain to fail. Similarly, we will turn people off if we call ourselves Christians but wear a long face. If we would draw people to Christ, we need to be excited about our Saviour. People need to see the joy in our faces in everyday living.

In 1 Peter 1:8–9, Peter encourages the saints about their faith in Jesus Christ: "Whom having not seen, ye love; in whom, though now ye see him not, yet believing, ye rejoice with joy unspeakable and full of glory: receiving the end of your faith, even the salvation of your souls."

Christ alone is our source of joy. If we depend on anyone or anything else to make us joyful, we will be disappointed. As we reflect on what Christ has done for us, making us partakers of His salvation, our problems fall into proper perspective. When we study His Word and draw close to Him, we find joy bubbling up within us.

Like David, we can say with confidence: "Thou hast made known to me the ways of life; thou shalt make me full of joy with thy countenance" (Acts 2:28).

So many people today are depressed, believing that life is hopeless. They don't know which way to turn for help. May we live so others can see our joy. Then we can share with them our source of joy—the Lord Jesus Christ.

I Found a Treasure

If you're searching for pleasure, for wealth, or for fame,
Or perpetual youth, a renowned family name,

But you find life is empty as the pleasures increase,
Then consider the Treasure who gives lasting peace.

I, too, was once hopeless, but I now have to sing,
For I've found a new life and it makes my heart ring.

Jesus Christ saved my soul and He's so dear to me;
I will praise Him forever, for His love set me free.

Christ, our Lord and our Saviour, was willing to go
To the cross where He suffered for the debt that I owed,

And He hung there alone till the debt was all paid,
Cruelly beaten and bruised, crucified and betrayed.

At an altar of prayer, I heard Christ call my name;
As I knelt there confessing my sin and my shame,

All my sins were forgiven, my heart was made clean,
And I found in my Treasure what happiness means.

Won't you come now and meet Him? You'll be so satisfied,
For His mercy's eternal, and His love multiplied.

You will never be sorry, for in Christ there abounds
Both the world's greatest Treasure and the best life around.

An Odd

As my husband and I were watching our five ducks, we noticed that one of them had been born with a deformity that caused him to hold his body at an unnatural angle. Alone, he stood at a distance from the others. While we watched, he approached the other ducks. At once, one of the four, with head lowered, ran at him, chasing him away. This happened several times. Clearly, they had rejected him. Although one duck seemed to be the leader, the rest followed his example, letting the odd duck know he was not wanted.

How often mankind acts like that. In ancient Athens, people sometimes singled out a person to be exiled because they viewed him as a threat to the state. People voted on whom to exile by writing the name of that person on pieces of broken pottery called *ostracon*. If one person received enough votes, he was banished, or ostracized. Usually this time of exile lasted ten years. From this practice is derived our word *ostracized*.

The Apostle John experienced this when he was exiled for his faithful testimony of Jesus Christ and the Word of God. He was sent to Patmos, a rocky, barren island fifteen miles in circumference. It was here that God revealed to John the visions concerning the condition of the churches and the end of the world. When the Emperor Domitian, who had banished John, died two years later, John was brought back to Ephesus where he had been bishop of the church. It is believed John was eighty years old at this time.

As Christians, we don't know what we may have to face in the future. We know that throughout the ages and until the present time, those who stand for the truth have faced persecution and death. Being shunned or ostracized is painful. We have the assurance, however, as did the Apostle John, that this world is not our home. Like Abraham, we look for a city whose builder and maker is God.

May we be encouraged when others see us as odd or different because of our testimony for Jesus Christ. Let's count it all joy to suffer for Jesus like the heroes of faith have done. If we endure unto the end, we will receive the crown of life. May the words of Revelation 14:12 be spoken of us: "Here is the patience of the saints: here are they that keep the commandments of God, and the faith of Jesus."

To Live or Die

When I read about the martyrs
Who for Jesus took a stand,
Though it cost them death or peril,
To obey the Lord's commands,

I must ask, "Have I the courage
That I need to see me through?
In such times of persecution,
Will I then be brave and true?"

Then I think of how my Saviour
Hung upon the cross for me,
And I blush at my reluctance
To endure adversity.

So I ask you, Lord, for courage
When the tests of life I face,
May I lean upon your mercy,
And rely upon your grace.

Give me faith that will not falter
In the midst of battles here,
That I'll stand in brave assurance
When the trials of faith appear.

Father, I would hold my station
When the enemy's in view,
For the only thing that matters
Is that I am true to you.

A Sweet Savor

Leviticus 1–3 outlines the laws for the meat, peace, and burnt offerings. These were offerings made by fire, offered as a sweet savor unto the Lord. What made them a sweet savor unto the Lord? It was the fact that they were offered as an act of obedience to God. The most important thing God expected of His people was obedience. When they followed God's commandments, they pleased God. When their hearts turned away from Him, even their offerings were an abomination to Him.

Psalm 51:10 outlines the conditions for proper worship of God: "Create in me a clean heart, O God; and renew a right spirit within me." Verse 17 says, "The sacrifices of God are a broken spirit: a broken and a contrite heart, O God, thou wilt not despise."

The offerings made by the Israelites were consumed by fire. I thought of the "fires" we might use to offer up a sacrifice to the Lord. Often the "fires" of tests, trials, and tribulations produce the sweetest savor. A *test* is "a basis for evaluating someone."[14] *Trial* is described as "a painful experience, an instance of trouble or hardship, especially one that tests one's ability to endure."[15] *Tribulation* is "a hardship, great difficulty, affliction, or distress, a cause of suffering."[16] When we go through these difficulties, God is watching us, noticing how we respond.

Psalm 66:10 says, "For thou, O God, hast proved us: thou hast tried us, as silver is tried." Abraham was tried when God told him to offer his son Isaac as a sacrifice, but he passed the test. God did not allow Abraham to slay his son, but provided a substitute.

1 Peter 1:7 gives us a window into God's purposes in allowing hard

times: ". . . that the trial of your faith, being much more precious than of gold that perisheth, though it be tried with fire, might be found unto praise and honour and glory at the appearing of Jesus Christ." When something is tried, its quality is proven. Through the experiences we face in life, our faith is tested to determine if it is effective, reliable, and true. When we come through like gold, our faith is a sweet savor unto God, well pleasing unto Him.

James 1:12 speaks of the reward of persevering in trials: "Blessed is the man that endureth temptation: for when he is tried, he shall receive the crown of life, which the Lord hath promised to them that love him." Proverbs 17:3 tells us, "The fining pot is for silver, and the furnace for gold: but the Lord trieth the hearts." The difficulties we face in our walk with God are to purify us and make us stronger. When we are faithful, staking our confidence on God, I believe He smiles at the sweet savor the "fires" have produced.

Through Fire

In trials and in testings
And tribulations sore,
When, Lord, our faith is tested,
We pray we'd love you more.

The furnace of affliction,
The fires that burn the dross,
Refine the gold and silver
That glorify your cross.

O bring us through triumphant,
Your saints in white array,
Resplendent in the garments
Of purity and grace.

Discouragement

I was already under lot of stress when I was diagnosed with diabetes. Discouragement pressed down, casting over me its shadows. I wanted to crawl away and hide, to forget my responsibilities and the needs of those who depended on me. It seemed I could focus only on my own needs, my own hurts. These hurts became magnified as I dwelt on them, which fed my self-pity.

In Numbers 21:4–5, the children of Israel were on their journey when "the soul of the people was much discouraged because of the way." They spoke against God, complaining about the manna He had given them to eat.

The things we encounter in life, like the things the Israelites encountered along the way, often discourage us. In my time of discouragement, the thoughts that no one understood, no one really cared, or no one else had experienced this, overcame me like a flood. Then an unexpected card came in the mail from someone saying, "I'm praying for you; I care."

Suddenly I realized that my focus had been wrong. I had prayed that God would change others, and change my situation. Now I began to pray that God would make me strong for Him wherever I found myself and that my life would glorify Him. As I switched my focus to Christ, I began to rise out of the mire of discouragement. I discovered that we will not remain discouraged long if we allow Christ to speak to us. I realized that the thoughts I had entertained were suggested by the father of lies. John 10:10 speaks of the thief, Satan, who comes "to steal, and to kill, and to destroy." Satan tries to discourage us, attempting to turn our focus away from Christ.

In Isaiah 41:10, God assures Israel that He will help them: "Fear thou not; for I am with thee: be not dismayed; for I am thy God: I will strengthen thee; yea, I will help thee; yea, I will uphold thee with the right hand of my righteousness." The word *dismay* in this verse means "a feeling of discouragement, hopelessness, disappointment, or a sudden loss of courage or confidence."[17]

We can take courage in knowing that God is here to help us. We can depend on Him at all times. How thankful I am also for faithful saints who listen to God's Spirit and minister to those in need. If we feel led to send a card, speak a word of encouragement, give a hug, pay a visit, or pray for someone, we should do it. Our small token of love may be just what another person needs to encourage her to look up and trust in the God who loves her.

Don't surrender to despair,
But look up to God who cares.

Where Is God?

My heart is numb, my mind aflame
With doubts and fears I cannot name.
My eyes are full, my spirit low,
Why must I grieve and suffer so?

Is there some point to all this pain?
I cannot see; Lord, make it plain.
I'm trying to be strong and brave,
But grief engulfs me like a wave.

Where are you, God? Or don't you care?
It's almost more than I can bear.
O Father, it's a deadly ache;
Restore my faith before I break.

And then I heard Him, "Child, I'm here,
I see your pain; I feel your fear;
My eyes have seen each tear you cried;
And I will never leave your side."

O blessed peace that filled my heart
To know that God would not depart.
Then hope awoke where grief had been;
I dried my eyes and smiled again.

Fear Not

Jeeps rumbled down our city streets, manned by the National Guard who carried loaded guns. It was 1967, and the city of Cincinnati, Ohio, where we lived, was the scene of race riots and vandalism. Local businesses were broken into, burned from fire bombs, and looted. The stores where we usually bought our groceries and did our laundry were now boarded up. The college where my husband attended had received several bomb threats. No one knew what would happen next. We used to walk the streets with our baby, but now it seemed unsafe to do so. Many people were paralyzed by fear.

Today we hear of gunmen shooting innocent school children, or terrorists setting off bombs to kill unsuspecting bystanders. These events send a wave of fear across the nation. Who will be the next victim?

History records man's cruelty toward others. Every war has claimed innocent lives. As long as this world stands, there will be people whose actions bring fear to others.

The words in our reading today were written by David when he was being sought by his enemies. David, however, did not give in to fear. Instead, he focused on God. He praised God, believing that God would hear his prayer and preserve him. Three times David stated that he would trust in the Lord and not be afraid. He could have allowed his fear to consume him, but he found comfort in the certainty that God was for him.

Jesus spoke to His disciples about fear. He knew they would be persecuted for His name's sake. After Christ's death, the disciples were huddled behind closed doors because they feared the Jews. After Christ arose, He appeared among them and spoke words they needed to hear: "Peace be unto you" (John 20:19). Again Jesus said, "Peace be unto you: as my Father hath sent me, even so send I you" (John 20:21). He did not want them to hide away in fear. He had a mission for them.

Some people are fearful of the last days. Jesus spoke about the signs of those days. Luke 21:26 talks about ". . . men's hearts failing them for fear, and for looking after those things which are coming on the earth: for the powers of heaven shall be shaken." Those whose hope and faith are not in Jesus will be consumed by fear. Christ reminds us in Luke 21:34 to be careful lest at any time our hearts become burdened down with the cares of this life and self-indulgence, making us unprepared for His coming.

In today's troublesome times, Christ does not want us to live in fear. He wants us to do as David did and put our trust in Him. He has a mission for each of us. Maybe it is to share with our neighbors the peace we have found, or to serve Him in some faraway place. Wherever we are, whoever we touch, we need to share with others how Christ delivers us from fear and gives us peace. May we say boldly with the Apostle Paul, "The Lord is my helper, and I will not fear what man shall do unto me" (Hebrews 13:6).

Fear Not, My Child

"Fear not, my child," Christ whispered;
I stilled myself to hear.
"Remember I am with you;
There's nothing here to fear."

"I'll trust you, Lord," I promised,
"When worry turns to dread;
And turn to you who gives me
Your blessed peace instead."

I'll fear no angry mortal,
For Christ my soul will shield.
Not even death can harm me;
My destiny is sealed.

Comparing
Ourselves

How well I remember my adolescent years. During those years I struggled with being different. I bemoaned the fact that I was large-boned, overweight, and on top of that, I had to wear glasses. Why wasn't I small-boned, tall, and slender like my older sister? Why did God make me like this?

At some time or other, we have all probably wished we could be like someone else—prettier, richer, more talented, or more successful. Sometimes these comparisons even pervade the church. We hear comments like: "I wish I could pray like that person, or explain the Word like that one."

2 Corinthians 10:12 reminds us, "For we dare not make ourselves of the number, or compare ourselves with some that commend themselves: but they measuring themselves by themselves, and comparing themselves among themselves, are not wise."

What are some results of comparing ourselves with others? First, it gives us an untrue or distorted view of ourselves and others. We should always do our best and give our best, but when we look at what others can do, we may become discouraged with our abilities.

Second, this comparison may make us feel like we are nothing, causing us to give up entirely, or it may bring feelings of envy. It may also stir up feelings of contempt toward someone whom we think does not measure up to us.

Third, when we compare ourselves with others, we may see all their faults or shortcomings, and fail to see our own. Thus, we feed pride instead of the humility we ought to cultivate.

Fourth, when we become dissatisfied with who we are, we say, in effect, that God did not know what He was doing when He created us. We show ungratefulness to God when we don't appreciate the gifts or talents He has given us. Doesn't He know everything about us? Isn't God actively present in our lives from conception to our death? Are we willing to acknowledge that He knows what is best for us?

Our talents, beauty, or whatever we have, are not the results of our merits, but gifts from God. Thus, we cannot take pride in them. As it says in 1 Corinthians 1:31, "He that glorieth, let him glory in the Lord."

Instead of comparing ourselves among ourselves, we should compare ourselves to God's measuring stick. His measure is always just, true, and revealing. It shows us what is in our hearts. David prayed these words: "Search me, O God, and know my heart: try me, and know my thoughts: and see if there be any wicked way in me, and lead me in the way everlasting" (Psalm 139:23–24).

May we not covet what God has given to another, but rejoice in the blessings He has given us. Being satisfied with who we are and what we have, and committing our lives to Christ is the way to find fulfillment and happiness. We must let the glory of our great God shine in our life to His honor and glory.

Discontentment

Do I ever look at someone,
And wish that I were she?
Or view with discontentment
This person that is me?

If I'd only be contented,
Lay comparisons aside,
And seek my Lord's approval,
My soul'd be satisfied.

For it's only God can see me
For who I really am,
Where hide, in hidden layers,
Those things that displease Him.

So I'll leave to Christ to measure
How short or tall I stand,
And remember I'm created
By God's almighty hand.

Giving Thanks

We were traveling through the Allegheny Mountains in West Virginia with two of our sons and their families when our son Michael noticed smoke coming from our van. As soon as he saw a place to pull off, he quickly parked and cried, "Everybody out!" Immediately we jumped out. We were losing transmission fluid, and a small fire had to be extinguished.

What were we to do? Since we didn't have any phone signal, we couldn't call for help, but our prayers ascended to our heavenly Father, and He heard our cries. One of the grandchildren wailed, "Why did this have to happen?"

I replied, "We don't know why, but remember the Bible says in 1 Thessalonians 5:18, 'In every thing give thanks: for this is the will of God in Christ Jesus concerning you.' Let's just thank Him that we are all safe, the fire is out, and we have food and water. God knows all about our trouble. Just trust Him."

Soon people began stopping. One was a mechanic who took my husband to get transmission fluid. A lady passed, and then came back. She said, "I don't have any loaves or fish, but I do have fruit bars." We assured her that we had food. After pouring in the fluid, we were on our way again.

We sang the songs, "God Is So Good," and "God Answers Prayer." Before too long, though, steam was billowing out from under the hood. We crossed the road to another pull-off. All fourteen of us bailed out again. The men decided we needed a tow truck. We now had a phone signal, so we changed our hotel reservations to the nearest town.

A couple stopped and offered to take some of us to the hotel. They also called for a tow truck. Then another lady said she would take our luggage and as many as could fit in her car. That left only Michael to ride in the tow truck.

Our God had provided so well for us. The next day, with a new radiator hose, we were able to continue on our way home to Indiana. We may never know why we experienced those inconveniences. Perhaps it was to show our grandchildren how God cares for His own. We do know that when we thank God in all things, we have peace and rest. One thing for sure, the grandchildren won't forget that trip with Grandpa and Grandma.

May we always remember the joy of thanking God and trusting Him in all circumstances. "Blessed be God, which hath not turned away my prayer, nor his mercy from me" (Psalm 66:20).

Without Number

I'll try to number all the ways
That God has blessed me night and day—

From childhood when I lisped a prayer
For God to keep me in His care

Till now when I am growing old—
And ponder sacred things, untold.

They fill my heart, my life, my soul;
My thoughts cannot contain the whole

Nor can my mind or heart expand
To speak what I can't understand,

Nor grasp the love of God for man,
Nor see that all is from His hand.

And yet, I'll strive to praise Him till
My lips are closed in death so still,

For Christ is all the world to me:
My life, my joy, my hope is He.

Though words may fail to clearly tell,
God knows my heart and all is well.

Be Strong

When my six sons were growing up, they often liked to arm wrestle. Sometimes they would ask, "Mom, will you arm wrestle me?" When they could finally defeat me, they felt elated at this proof of their strength. As their mother, I realized my sons were becoming strong young men.

In Ephesians 6:10, Paul admonishes us, "Be strong in the Lord, and in the power of his might." Then he tells us how to attain this strength—we must put on the armor that Christ provides for us. Paul warns us that we need this armor to resist the temptations of Satan. In our own strength, we are unable to defeat the powers of evil.

Verse 12 says we do not wrestle against flesh and blood; rather, we wage a spiritual battle against the devil and his cohorts. We need the armor of God to equip us for the encounter with evil. First, we need to have the belt of truth around us. Second, we must put on the breastplate of righteousness—not our righteousness, but Christ's. Third, we need to have our feet shod with the preparation of the Gospel of peace. Fourth, we must don the helmet of salvation. Fifth, we arm ourselves with the sword of the Spirit, which is the Word of God. Finally, we must not forget to pray all the time, asking God to protect us and intervene on our behalf. We are commanded to pray, not only for ourselves, but for all Christians everywhere. There is much power in prayer. This is one way we can help other believers, even those whom we do not know.

Paul asked the Ephesians to pray for him as he suffered in prison. He felt the need of the saints' prayers so he could be bold for the Lord.

Paul realized his own strength was not equal to the task. He needed the Lord's strength and the support of other Christians.

Let's clothe ourselves with the armor of God each day so we can go forth to live for Christ through His power and strength. The only way to victorious living is to put on the armor of God. The arm of flesh will not be able to prevail against the enemy. Let's trust and obey and be strong in the Lord.

O Praise His Name

O Lord, I falter on my way;
My strength is frail, and yet
I know in you the power is found
To keep me day by day.

I need to only call your name,
And tell you of my need,
And you're right there to strengthen me;
There's power in Jesus' name!

How can I think that I know best
The path that I should walk
When I can't see what lies ahead,
The pitfalls and the tests.

God, I surrender all my life;
I crown you Lord and King,
For you alone can lead me home
Through all this earthly strife.

I praise you, Glorious Lamb who died,
To save my soul from death,
To lift me out of sin and self,
And hold me by your side.

"Lord, Save Us"

In today's reading, Jesus and His disciples were out on the sea when a great storm arose. Jesus lay asleep, even when the storm grew so strong that the ship was swamped by the waves. The disciples feared for their lives. They didn't know what to do. Finally they ran to wake Jesus, crying, "Lord, save us: we perish" (Matthew 8:25).

Jesus calmly asked, "Why are you so afraid? Where is your faith?" Then Jesus arose and rebuked the storm with these words, "Peace, be still" (Mark 4:39). The winds obeyed their Master, and the sea became calm.

The disciples marveled, wondering what manner of man this was whom even the winds and the sea obeyed. Why did they marvel? Hadn't they seen Jesus heal the sick, the lame, the blind, and the lepers? How could they not have great faith in Him? They did not yet understand that they were safe when Jesus was with them. Was the storm a test of their faith?

We should not be too critical of the disciples, for how often do we panic when we face storms and tests? Do we forget that Christ is with us? Do we think we have to handle things on our own? We try to, don't we? Then we realize that without the Saviour's help, we, too, will perish. May we ask God to increase our faith and trust in Him. When the winds and waves are tossing us about, how thankful we can be that our Lord is there. When our fear is great, we can call out to Jesus for help, and He hears. He will calm our sea, bringing peace to our souls.

The Storm

Based on Mark 4:36–40

On a mighty raging sea,
Where the waves rose recklessly,
The disciples' ship was rocked,
While the heartless tempest mocked.

As the waves intensified,
Bolts of lightning filled the sky,
And as water filled the boat,
They despaired to stay afloat.

On a pillow, sound asleep,
Lay the Master of the deep.
"Wake up, Master, don't you care
If we perish way out here?"

From His slumber, Jesus woke,
He arose and calmly spoke
To the winds, and they obeyed;
All was calm, the tempest stayed.

Then He looked upon His men,
Who were marveling at Him,
"O my friends, why did you fear,
When you knew that I was here?"

The Rock

Lord, plant my feet upon the Rock
That's loftier than I.
Secure, I'll rest within your arms;
On you I can rely.

Lord, plant my feet upon the Rock,
And help me there to stand,
Though buffeted by wind or wave,
Till daylight is at hand.

Lord, plant my feet upon the Rock,
That's mightier than I,
For not a storm can shake me when
The Master's standing by.

Scripture reading: Jonah 1:1–7

Swallowed
or Surrendered?

Have you ever wanted to run away from your duties and responsibilities? I wondered, as I watched my widowed mother give round-the-clock care to my grandmother. She cared for her through dementia and the bedridden years until Grandma died. During this time, Mom was unable to go to church, except for the times when we visited and I stayed with Grandma.

I'm sure there were days or nights when my mother would have liked to lay it all down for a while, but she did not. She surrendered her life to God's will. In Him, she found the strength to love and serve her mother and her God.

Sometimes the things we're called to do may feel insignificant. We can't imagine how our efforts will make a difference. Do you suppose that is how the prophet Jonah felt when God called him to go preach to Nineveh?

Nineveh was a very wicked city; perhaps Jonah didn't think they would repent even if he preached to them. Maybe Jonah felt like they deserved God's wrath because they were so evil. Whatever rationale he used, Jonah decided to ignore God's command. He boarded a ship heading the opposite direction. God, however, knew exactly where Jonah was.

God sent a mighty storm that put those on board the ship in great danger. The sailors tried to lighten their ship by throwing off their goods, but all to no avail. They cried out to their gods, but still the storm raged. In desperation, they wakened Jonah and asked him to pray to his God for help. They cast lots to see whose sin God was punishing with this angry storm. The lot fell on Jonah. He admitted his guilt and told them to throw him overboard. Although they didn't want to, they finally conceded. As Jonah sank beneath the waves, the storm ceased, and the sea became calm.

God had prepared a great fish to swallow Jonah. He remained in the belly of this fish for three days and three nights. In Jonah 2:5, he writes, "The waters compassed me about, even to the soul: the depth closed me round about, the weeds were wrapped about my head." In verse 7, he testifies, "When my soul fainted within me I remembered the LORD: and my prayer came in unto thee, into thine holy temple." Jonah realized his only hope was in God. The prayer he offered in the depths of the ocean soared all the way to God in His holy temple. Jonah had come to the end of himself. He was willing to stop running and to obey God's call. He surrendered to God's will. After God caused the fish to spew Jonah out on dry land, Jonah went and preached to Nineveh. The whole city repented, escaping the wrath of God.

We, too, must surrender our lives to God. If we disobey, God will use the Holy Spirit to prod us, convict us, and reveal His will to us. Only in surrendering everything to God can we find peace. Whether His will is for us to have pleasant days or days that try us, we can depend on His grace and strength. We know He will not give us more than we can bear. He has promised to make a way of escape for us. God is always faithful.

Hear and Obey

God has a work for us to do,
Great it may be or small.
Our task is to attend, obey,
And waiver not at all.

If He should send us far away
To share the Gospel light,
Or bid, instead, we work at home,
We'll be His candle bright.

It matters not the time or place,
The work we're called to do,
But that we're faithful to the end,
And Jesus finds us true.

Scripture reading: Colossians 3:22–25

Do Your *Best*

I suppose we have all had days when everything seemed to go wrong. Maybe the washer spewed water on the floor, soaking the clothes waiting to be washed and the baby who was crawling through them. Perhaps there were too many things that needed to be done, and it seemed impossible to accomplish them all. Or maybe a sick child claimed our attention, and we had to put aside other things, including cleaning our messy house.

Often on one of those trying days I would hear a cheery *hello* and look up to see my mother-in-law at the door. Invariably, I would glance at the clutter around me and the children clinging to my skirt and think, "What is she going to think of me now?" Her house was always clean and clutter-free. However, she seemed to understand. Maybe she had once had days like that too.

Finally, I learned that if I was doing my best in the situation in which I found myself, I did not need to berate myself. One person can only do so much. I needed to put first things first. A sick baby definitely deserves precedence over household duties. I found that cleaning was more manageable if I tackled at least one or two cleaning jobs each day rather than leaving all the cleaning for one day.

Doing our best is a habit that we need to pursue in all we do, not just in our household and family responsibilities. Sometimes mothers, especially those with young children, may feel like their lives are insignificant because they don't have much time out of the house. But we have a vital task—the task of teaching our children. Teaching them by example and word is important.

Although the timing of my mother-in-law's visits was not always the most convenient, the Lord gave me grace to greet her cheerfully. As I sought to make her feel welcome, prepare a meal for her, or just listen to her, I learned an important lesson. My house, and how it looked, was not what she really cared about, but rather the respect and attention I gave her. In her eighties she was stricken with cancer. I watched as she grew frail. When I sat beside her bed as she was dying, I was glad I had done my best to treat her well. I had grown to love her over the years. I was thankful I had spoken to her of her relationship with Christ and of my love for her.

We may not always know the effects of doing our best, but God sees, and He will reward us. Wherever we are in life, whatever the tasks we are called to do, may we do our best and do it for God's glory. When we are faithful in little, God will entrust us with greater responsibilities. If in all things we do our best, doing it as unto Jesus, He will receive the glory, and we will be blessed.

A Work for Us to Do

We may not be like David
Who mighty giant slew,
But Jesus has assignments
For each of us to do.

It may be words of kindness
That lift another's load,
Or prayers beseeching courage
To others on life's road.

Those tiny acts of service
We do throughout the day,
If done for love of Jesus,
All serve a noble aim.

For every cup of water,
Dispensed in Jesus' name,
Will bless both heir and giver,
And glorify God's name.

We may be called to labor
In land that's far away,
Or serve upon the home front;
The value is the same.

When comes the final harvest,
And Christ receives our sheaves,
Will we have grain to offer,
Or dry and crumpled leaves?

God Thinks
of Me

How often do we feel like no one understands us or cares that we even exist? While that might be true about people sometimes, it is never true of our loving Lord.

Psalm 139 is one of my favorite psalms because it shows us how well God knows us and how often He thinks of us. God gets quite personal with us in this chapter. In verse 1, it says He has searched us and known us. God does not look at our outward appearance. He looks deep within us and sees our thoughts, our desires, and our sins. God sees our entire self—who we actually are.

In verse 3, we read that He is acquainted with all our ways. Verse 4 says that God knows our thoughts even before we voice them. In verse 16, we see that God knew us even before we were completely formed in our mother's womb. In verses 17 and 18 the psalmist exclaims, "How precious also are thy thoughts unto me, O God! how great is the sum of them! If I should count them, they are more in number than the sand."

Psalm 40:5 says, "Many, O LORD my God, are thy wonderful works which thou hast done, and thy thoughts which are to us-ward: they cannot be reckoned up in order unto thee: if I would declare and speak of them, they are more than can be numbered." We are always in God's thoughts.

When I consider how important we are to God, I think of John 3:16: "For God so loved the world, that he gave his only begotten Son, that whosoever believeth in him should not perish, but have everlasting life." How can we feel unloved or neglected when God was willing to give His only Son to die for us?

Psalm 33:18 reads, "Behold, the eye of the LORD is upon them that fear him, upon them that hope in his mercy." We must keep our focus on Jesus, fear Him, trust Him, and put our hope in Him.

We can take comfort in the thought that we are never forgotten by God. As the psalmist says in Psalm 40:17: "But I am poor and needy; yet the Lord thinketh upon me: thou art my help and my deliverer; make no tarrying, O my God." We can cry out to God when we feel unloved, discouraged, or unnoticed. After all, He knows us, loves us, and He will hear our prayer for help. God is thinking of us. We are not alone.

When I think about how much God loves us, I can't help but love Him more. Somehow, I believe that is what He hopes will happen. Let's not forget God's thoughts toward us as we turn our thoughts to Him.

Jesus Knows Me

I've learned of famous kings,
From pictures that I see,
Yet I am fairly sure
They haven't heard of me.

But there's a mighty King
Renowned in wealth and fame,
Who cares about my soul—
He even knows my name.

He knows my every thought;
He hears my whispered prayers,
He holds me in His arms;
I know He really cares.

He thinks of me with love,
With thoughts that, like the sand,
Pervasive and sublime,
Extend throughout the land.

Though here I'm overlooked
By rulers rich or fine,
I'm loved by God above,
The King Supreme, Divine.

When We Don't Understand

When we are carrying a heavy load and we don't understand why, there is only one solution. We must give it all to Jesus. He is the only One who understands what we are going through. Can we hand over our battle, our burden, our grief, our pain, our distress? Can we give it all to Jesus?

Jesus knows why we are distressed. He knows the pain we feel. He knows how frustrated we feel. God knows we are helpless creatures. Although we are weak, unable to stand alone, insufficient to bear the burden, His arms are strong. We must give it to Jesus and not try to fight the battle alone. Jesus will give us peace in the midst of trouble. He will calm our minds and souls. He will also allow us to find joy in spite of the trials we face.

Too often we badger God with the question "Why?" We must ask God to help us accept His wisdom and say, "Thy will be done." Let's open our hearts to God so He can show us what He wants to teach us through these experiences. Perhaps He wants to teach us patience or show us how to comfort and encourage others. Maybe He wants to make us stronger so we are prepared for greater trials ahead.

When I lost my fifteen-year-old brother in a car accident, I couldn't understand why God would take someone so young. Two years later, my father and grandfather both passed away. I grieved that my children would never know them. I had three children and was four and a half months pregnant when I suffered a miscarriage. When we realized we had lost twin girls, I felt devastated. But God was still God. He was there for us even in the hard times. A few years later, my mother had a brain tumor, and after surgery, communication with her became impossible. She endured the afflictions of her body for four years before she was released to go to her Lord.

We may never know why we face these trials, but God knows, and that will have to be enough for now. Can we learn to lean on Christ, trusting His everlasting arms to hold us? Someday we'll understand that His plan for us was better than any we could have chosen. When we think things are too hard for us, or the temptations too strong to resist, let's claim the promise in 1 Corinthians 10:13, "There hath no temptation taken you but such as is common to man: but God is faithful who will not suffer you to be tempted above that ye are able; but will with the temptation also make a way to escape, that ye may be able to bear it."

May we never doubt the love of God. In Hebrews 2:17, we see that our Lord is a merciful and faithful High Priest who intercedes to God for us. Because He has suffered and faced temptation, He is able to deliver us in our temptations. Hebrews 4:15 reminds us that Christ is touched by our infirmities. In verse 16, we are invited, "Let us therefore come boldly to the throne of grace, that we may obtain mercy, and find grace to help in time of need." God has not left us helpless or defenseless against the enemy of our soul. Even when we don't understand, God is with us.

Trust

I may not understand, but Lord, I'll trust you,
Although the way is dark, and I can't see.
I know you'll hold my hand and guide my footsteps.
I need not fear the night, for you're with me.

So when the trials come, and I am tempted
To take the easy way, Lord, make me strong.
And give me faith enough to keep on trusting,
To walk the narrow path, to shun the wrong.

Lord, I may never know why you have chosen
This overwhelming load for me to bear,
But this I know for sure: that you are with me;
I feel your loving touch; I know you care.

For every trial, I've found there's grace unmeasured;
In every storm of life, you calm the sea.
You hold me in your arms, a precious treasure;
And there I'll rest for all eternity.

So I will walk each day in full surrender.
I'll trust the way you lead is always best.
My heart and life is yours; you know the future.
Contentment in your arms is perfect rest.

Contend for
the Faith

*I*n a day when sin is not called sin and immorality is common-place, how do we respond? Do we become calloused to the flagrant disregard of God's Word? Do we try to isolate ourselves from those with whom we differ? Are we fearful of retribution if we speak out against the sin that is taking over our world?

This is not a new challenge. Sin has wreaked havoc ever since Adam and Eve disobeyed God. In the Old Testament, God sent prophets to warn people of His judgment because of their sin. Some, like the people of Nineveh, repented, but many did not. Only Lot and his two daughters escaped the destruction of Sodom and Gomorrah, and that because of the prayers of righteous Abraham. Jesus asks in Luke 18:8, "When the Son of man cometh, shall he find faith on the earth?"

Galatians 3:26–27 tells us, "For ye are all the children of God by faith in Christ Jesus. For as many of you as have been baptized into Christ have put on Christ." In Ephesians 4:4–6 we read: "There is one body, and one Spirit, even as ye are called in one hope of your calling; one Lord, one faith, one baptism, one God and Father of all, who is above all, and through all, and in you all." John 3:36 promises, "He that believeth on the Son hath everlasting life: and he that believeth not the Son shall not see life; but the wrath of God abideth on him."

This is the faith for which we are to earnestly contend. *Contend* comes from the Latin word *contendere,* meaning "to strive together."[18] The church of Jesus Christ must strive together to keep the faith. We

274

are one body, and need to encourage each other to be faithful and true to Christ and His teachings. As we see end times approaching, we need a faith that will stand, that will not shrink in the face of opposition, oppression, or persecution.

Many saints throughout the years have willingly laid down their lives for their faith in Jesus Christ. Is our faith as dear to us as theirs was to them? Do we teach our children to love Jesus? Do we show them by our actions and words that Jesus means the world to us? Do they understand that the Bible is the Word of God and that it is precious to us? Do they see evidence in our lives that our faith in Jesus is worth dying for?

Only when our relationship with Christ is vibrant and alive are we able to convey the importance of our faith to others. Let's contend for the faith. May we make it known that we believe in Jesus and that all His words are truth. Let's not be deceived, for in the last days, except for God's grace, even the elect would be deceived. Let's keep the faith and share it with others.

Jude encouraged the church with these words, "But ye, beloved, building up yourselves on your most holy faith, praying in the Holy Ghost, keep yourselves in the love of God, looking for the mercy of our Lord Jesus Christ unto eternal life" (Jude 20–21). May we say as Paul did, "I have fought a good fight, I have finished my course, I have kept the faith: Henceforth there is laid up for me a crown of righteousness" (2 Timothy 4:7–8).

Hold Fast the Faith

The martyrs, truth did not forsake,
But gave their all for Jesus' sake;
Their love for Christ compelled them to
His Word obey, His will pursue.

Yet we who dwell in freedom here,
Who have so little cause for fear,
Are sorely pressed to touch the cross
Or risk enduring any loss.

What will Christ say on Judgment Day
If we forsake the narrow way?
If we have been ashamed of Him,
He'll say aloud, "I don't know them."

O give us, Lord, a passion great,
A love for you that won't abate;
May we stand firm, devoted, true,
To everything that's dear to you.

May we not shrink from anything,
But through it all, your praises sing.
Lord, give us grace to simply trust
The truth that you'll be here for us,

And keep the faith that sets us free,
That from our sins brings liberty;
Oh, help us, Lord, a crown to win,
And cling to Jesus till the end.

When the Dark
Billows Roll

*I*f sailors are out on a lake or the ocean and a fierce storm arises, they might see waves so high that they make the vessel seem small. Add to these threatening waves a dark night with no moonlight or stars shining. As the waves and wind toss the vessel, and water pours in, what can they do?

The Apostle Paul was in a situation like this. Paul, along with his fellow prisoners, was being taken to Italy. For several days, they saw neither sun nor stars, and the relentless wind did not let up. After tossing overboard everything they could, the men resigned themselves to death. However, Paul encouraged them, saying God had spoken to him through an angel (Acts 27:23–24). Paul informed them that the angel had said they would be shipwrecked on a certain island, but that all their lives would be saved. On the fourteenth night, they discovered they were indeed near an island. Although they had been fasting, now Paul told them to eat, and he gave thanks to God. As they tried to get closer to land, they ran aground, and the back of the ship was broken by violent waves. Each man grabbed something to hold onto and they all made it safely to shore.

Haven't all of us been in circumstances over which we had no control? Sometimes these crises can seem as overwhelming as those dark billows which Paul faced. What do we do? Where do we turn? Paul was at ease, for he knew who was in control of the waves. He knew God could have calmed the winds as He did on the Sea of Galilee for the disciples, but He didn't.

God had a different plan. Perhaps He wanted the captain and prisoners to see what God could do for them. Or maybe He intended to use the shipwreck as a means of proclaiming the Gospel to the inhabitants of this island. The islanders watched when a poisonous snake fastened itself onto Paul's arm, and he shook it off into the fire without being harmed. The people were amazed. They thought Paul was a god. When Paul laid hands on the chief's father and he was healed, others also came for healing. For three months Paul preached to these people, as the shipwrecked party waited for a ship to rescue them. Paul's "dark billows" experience was used to glorify God. Paul had given himself wholly to God, to be used however He wished. Paul was sold out to God, no matter what suffering came his way. This shipwreck was only one of Paul's many trials of faith (2 Corinthians 11:25–28).

When the dark billows threaten our life, we can remember Paul, who counted it all joy to suffer for His Lord. We must get our eyes off ourselves and fix them on Jesus, who is able to deliver us, no matter how high the waves or how dark the night.

When the Waves Roll

When the billows wash over my soul,
And they threaten to sweep me away,
I will trust, and will not be afraid;
For I know that my Lord's in control.

Though the tempests may buffet and blow,
And the darkness overshadow the way,
I will trust in my Captain always,
He alone knows the right way to go.

Precious friend, are you trying to row
In a boat that is sore overwhelmed?
Let the Lord have control of your helm;
He will keep you from plunging below.

*P*risoners

ne windy fall day my two preschool children were playing outside. From time to time I glanced out the window to see where they were. It was nearly lunchtime when I realized I had not heard them for a while. Deciding I'd better call them for lunch, I hurried outside.

I looked around, calling their names as I walked. Neither seeing nor hearing them made me a little anxious. "Lord," I prayed, "where are they?" I headed toward a shed that they had claimed for their play-house. As I noticed it was locked, my hopes sank. Again, I called, my voice competing with the wind.

There, did I hear something? Yes, I did! Reaching the shed, I released the bar that locked the door. The door opened, and my children tumbled out. Their words poured out as they both tried to explain what had happened.

The strong wind had blown over the stick they had used to prop the door open, and the bar had fallen into place, holding them prisoners in the shed. "We called and called, Mommy, but you couldn't hear us. Then we prayed to Jesus that you would come looking for us, and you did. Jesus heard our prayers, and answered them, didn't He?"

I assured them that He surely had heard and answered. We thanked God for hearing their cries to Him. Psalm 34:15 affirms, "The eyes of the LORD are upon the righteous, and his ears are open to their cry." The Lord saw my children locked in that shed, and His ears heard their fervent cry. He saw their faith in Him and answered their prayers for help.

God hears us, too, whatever our need. Maybe we are prisoners to sin or bad habits. The psalmist says in Psalm 102:1–2, "Hear my prayer, O LORD, and let my cry come unto thee. Hide not thy face from me in the day when I am in trouble; incline thine ear unto me: in the day when I call answer me speedily." In Psalm 56:13, David testifies, "For thou hast delivered my soul from death: will not thou deliver my feet from falling, that I may walk before God in the light of the living?" David put his trust in God; so can we. When we call, He will answer. In our mighty God is deliverance.

O Praise the Lord

O praise the Lord, for He is good,
He knows our needs before we call.
He feeds our souls with heavenly food,
And lifts us up when we would fall.

O praise the Lord for He is great,
He knows that we are weak and frail.
His certain help is never late,
Nor will His promise ever fail.

The Lord's
Battle

*I*n 2 Chronicles 20 we read a thrilling story of victory. Jehoshaphat, the king of Judah, had just received word that a great army was launching an attack against him. Afraid, he proclaimed a fast for all the people. They gathered in the house of the Lord to seek Him. Their prayer is recorded in verse 6: "O LORD God of our fathers, art not thou God in heaven? and rulest not thou over all the kingdoms of the heathen? and in thy hand is there not power and might, so that none is able to withstand thee?" They confessed their faith in God and in His power. In verse 9, they proclaimed that when they cry unto God in their affliction, God will hear and help.

As they stood before the Lord, Jahaziel prophesied, "Be not afraid nor dismayed by reason of this great multitude; for the battle is not yours, but God's" (2 Chronicles 20:15). He announced that the people would not even have to fight: "Set yourselves, stand ye still, and see the salvation of the LORD with you" (2 Chronicles 20:17). King Jehoshaphat and all the people fell before the Lord and worshiped Him. They praised God with a loud voice, believing He would bring victory.

When we are facing a battle, where do we go? What do we do? Is our first response to fast and pray, looking to God? Or do we try to fight the battle on our own? God wants us to come to Him. He knows that on our own we are not strong enough to win. Satan is much stronger than we are, but, praise God, our Lord is mightier than all! He wants us to give the battle over to Him.

The next morning, Jehoshaphat encouraged the people to believe in God. Then he appointed singers to go ahead of the army to praise God in the beauty of holiness, saying, "Praise the Lord; for his mercy endureth forever" (2 Chronicles 20:21). When they began to sing and to praise, the Lord defeated their enemies by setting ambushes against them. For three days the people stripped the slain of their riches. They returned home to Jerusalem with joy. They came with psalteries, harps, and trumpets to the house of the Lord, praising Him for His faithfulness. The fear of God was upon all the kingdoms around them when they heard how the Lord had fought against the enemies of Judah.

The enemy tries to make us think there is no hope. But God will not forsake us. In Psalm 4:1, David beseeches God to hear him. Later, in verses 4–5 of the same psalm, he admonishes us: "Stand in awe, and sin not . . . Offer the sacrifices of righteousness, and put your trust in the LORD."

Psalm 5:11–12 says, "But let all those that put their trust in thee rejoice: let them ever shout for joy, because thou defendest them: let them also that love thy name be joyful in thee. For thou, LORD, wilt bless the righteous; with favour wilt thou compass him as with a shield." May we always remember, the battle is not ours, but God's. Let's trust Him!

Cry to God

When the strife around us rages,
And we don't know where to turn,
We can cry to God for rescue,
For the battle's His concern.

He will rout the foes who'd harm us;
He will bring a victory grand
When we trust Him with the battle,
And we yield to His command.

So remember that the battle
Is the Lord's to fight, not ours.
We have neither strength nor wisdom,
God has all within His power.

Yea, the Lord of Hosts will conquer
Any foe that crosses us.
He is King of all the ages,
And He's worthy of our trust.

An Overcomer

When our oldest son Mark was about twelve, my husband bought a Jersey cow to provide milk for our growing family. We ran into a problem, however. This little cow was a kicker. Every time my husband tried to milk her, she would kick, dumping whatever milk was in the bucket. My husband wasn't too happy. Then our son asked if he could try to milk her. My husband told him to go ahead. Mark stayed alert for her kicks, but he did not give up. He focused on her, learning to anticipate her moves. He was determined to overcome this dilemma. Soon he was milking that cow without a problem, although he was the only one who could manage her.

The Bible contains glorious promises for those who overcome. In 1 John 2:13–15, John writes to all Christians, whatever their degree of spiritual maturity. Some were babes in Christ, some were mature Christians, and others were strong adults who had overcome the enemy. They had the Word of God abiding in them. All needed John's warning about how to relate to the world, however, if they would experience ongoing victory in their walk with Christ.

Just as my son had to focus on that cow to gain the victory over her, so we must focus on Christ, not allowing other things to distract us from Him. The Apostle John shows us how to examine our loves in 1 John 2:15: "Love not the world, neither the things that are in the world. If any man love the world, the love of the Father is not in him." In verse 16, he defines what it is we are not to love: "For all that is in the world, the lust of the flesh, and the lust of the eyes, and the pride of life, is not of the Father, but is of the world." In verse 17, John helps us gain an eternal perspective: "And the world passeth away, and the lust thereof: but he that doeth the will of God abideth for ever."

Christ calls us to overcome. That means there are battles to be faced and won. If we take our eyes off the prize, we cannot be victorious. When we get caught up in this world and all its allurements, we are headed for destruction.

Christ did not call us to an easy life. He calls us to endure hardness, to remain steadfast through struggles, and to resist the onslaughts of the enemy. Remember, though, it is not through our own strength that we conquer, but through our faith in Jesus Christ (1 John 5:4).

God gives several promises to those who overcome. In Revelation 2:7, Christ says that he who overcomes will be able to eat of the tree of life in the midst of the paradise of God. Verse 17 promises that the one who overcomes will be given hidden manna to eat and a white stone on which a new name is written. Verse 26 says, "And he that overcometh, and keepeth my works unto the end, to him I will give power over the nations." In verse 28, we read how the one who overcomes will be given the morning star.

In Revelation 3:5, the one who overcomes is promised white raiment, and that Christ will confess his name before the Father and His angels. Verse 12 says that Christ will write upon him the name of His God, a new name, and the name of the New Jerusalem. Christ says in verse 21 that the overcomer will sit with Him on His throne. Revelation 21:7 holds out to us a glorious promise: "He that overcometh shall inherit all things; and I will be his God, and he shall be my son."

Any price we may have to pay here will be worth it in the end. We must not allow the things of this world to drag us down. Let's be strong in the Lord, and overcome!

Saints, Awaken

All saints of God, awaken, and rise up to the call.
A battle fierce is raging; God's asking for your all.

We cannot be complacent as souls around are lost;
We need to win the battle, no matter what the cost.

We've enemies to fight and victories to win,
For precious human souls await release from sin.

The devil must be routed, the Spirit be obeyed,
And we'll see souls repenting to walk the narrow way.

Awake, and join the battle, and fight for God today.
Put on the Gospel armor and do not be dismayed,

For Christ will give us courage to go forth in His name;
With Jesus as our Captain, the victory we will claim.

All saints of God, awaken, and rise up to the call.
Christ wants us to be workers, so we must give our all.

Ask God to place a burden upon our hearts today,
That we may seek to rescue the souls that come our way.

God's Promises

*J*eremiah 31:11 tells us, "For the LORD hath redeemed Jacob, and ransomed him from the hand of him that was stronger than he." In this chapter, Jeremiah is speaking of how God will restore Israel. In verse 3, the Lord says, "Yea, I have loved thee with an everlasting love: therefore with lovingkindness have I drawn thee."

God promises great things to His special people. Although the Israelites were scattered into many lands, God said He would redeem them and bring them back to their land. Because of their disobedience, God had allowed other nations to conquer them. Most of His people were taken into captivity. God did this to teach the children of Israel that they could not continue in disobedience. Yet He promised that a remnant would be preserved to return to Israel.

God has redeemed us through Jesus Christ. We were held by Satan, and the chains that bound us were strong. But, praise God, Christ is stronger than Satan. Through our faith in Jesus, we have been set free. We are no longer bound by the chains of sin.

In Jeremiah 31:12, God gave the people three promises regarding their return to Zion. The first promise was that they would have all they needed—wheat, wine, and oil. These symbolized their physical prosperity. Second, Jeremiah speaks of their soul, promising it would be as a watered garden. A watered garden is one that is well cared for, sown in fertile soil, nourished by the rain, and producing fruit. The third promise is that they would not sorrow anymore. Their time of mourning would be over, for they would be at home in Zion.

How does this relate to us today? When we have Christ in our hearts, we have joy. The trials of this life cannot dim our joy or destroy our peace. In Christ we have all we need. Our soul is fed by streams of living water and nourished by God's love, bringing forth fruit. We also have the promise of a glorious future in heaven, where all sorrow will be banned. As Revelation 21:4 says, "And God shall wipe away all tears from their eyes; and there shall be no more death, neither sorrow, nor crying, neither shall there be any more pain: for the former things are passed away."

Even as the Israelites looked forward to returning to Jerusalem with the hope that their children could again inherit the land, we as Christians look forward to obtaining an inheritance. Revelation 21:7 says, "He that overcometh shall inherit all things; and I will be his God, and he shall be my son." The condition to meet is to be an overcomer. We must be faithful to Christ unto the end.

We find encouragement in Revelation 22:14: "Blessed are they that do his commandments, that they may have right to the tree of life, and may enter in through the gates into the city." Revelation 21:23 describes the city in fuller detail: "And the city had no need of the sun, neither of the moon, to shine in it: for the glory of God did lighten it, and the Lamb is the light thereof." May we cling to the promises of God and be faithful to Christ. God will give us grace to overcome if we look to Him.

I Have a Friend

I have a dear, beloved Friend
Who's never failed to care for me.
Since I believed, He's been my hope,
The Saviour of humanity.

I read His Word and feel His love;
His promises are steadfast, sure.
I'll trust Him in the storms that come;
His Word eternally endures.

No one has ever loved me so.
Throughout my life, I've found Him true;
He'll take me to His heavenly home.
When all my days on earth are through.

Security

I surveyed the army of fruit and vegetable jars standing like sentinels on the shelves in front of me. My family and I had worked hard to prepare and preserve them. With seven children in the family—all but one of them boys—we went through a lot of food. Knowing we had prepared well for the winter gave me a sense of security.

Later that winter my husband's work days were cut back. Where was my security now? How would we pay the bills? We prayed, and looked at our belongings. What could we sell to get some cash? I unloaded my china hutch with its pretty dishes, and sold it to meet our obligations.

During that time various people, some whom we didn't know well, brought us food staples or a gift of money. We survived that bleak period, but I learned a lesson. We can do all that is possible to be self-sufficient and provide security for our family, but the best security we can find is to put ourselves in God's care. When the props are knocked out from beneath us, we can still feel the everlasting arms of God holding us up.

I remember the Christmas day we returned home to find smoke coming from somewhere near our house. When we arrived, our barn was completely gone. We were thankful it was our barn and not our house. We never found out what started the fire, but it reminded us that the things of this life are temporary. We cannot retain them in our grasp.

Many people look to their savings, stocks, bonds, good health, or abilities to provide security for themselves and their loved ones. Yes, we should be thrifty, use our money wisely, and appreciate our health and the gifts God has given us, but we should do all this with the knowledge that those things can and do fail.

Jesus rebuked the people who followed Him merely because He had fed them. He admonished them not to labor for the meat that perishes (the things of this life), but to seek after the meat that endures to eternal life (John 6:27). He went on to tell them that He was the Bread from God that would give life to the world. In John 6:40, Jesus promised, "Every one which seeth the Son, and believeth on him, may have everlasting life: and I will raise him up at the last day."

Jesus is our security. Our life is short on this earth, and we can take nothing with us when we leave. However, if we believe in Christ and look to Him for forgiveness, He will abide with us. Then we can know that when this life is over, we will be secure in Him. We will have a home with Him forever.

Christ is the only source of true security. All else will fail and pass away. Can we not trust Him to care for His own? Psalm 146:5 tells us, "Happy is he that hath the God of Jacob for his help, whose hope is in the LORD his God." Psalm 118:8 reminds us, "It is better to trust in the LORD than to put confidence in man."

Whatever comes to us, may we remember that we are never forsaken. Our mighty God is with us and will keep us. We must not waver in faith, but believe in the One who loves and cares for us.

I Won't Worry

I won't worry about tomorrow;
I'll just live from day to day,
For I'm trusting in my Saviour
Who's beside me all the way.

So whatever life may bring me,
Be it joy, or sorrow great,
I believe I'll find His mercy
If I trust in Him and wait.

In the times I feel forsaken,
I'll remember God's still there.
And I'll feel His arms about me
When I come to Him in prayer.

Though the storms may howl around me,
And temptations threaten me,
I will trust God's keeping presence,
And His warm security.

I won't worry about the future,
For God's hands are strong and sure;
I am under His protection,
And His promises endure.

There is nothing can befall me,
But the Father sees it all.
And I know He guards my footsteps,
For He sees the sparrow fall.

"My Peace I Leave You"

The psalmist David said, "I will both lay me down in peace, and sleep: for thou, LORD, only makest me dwell in safety" (Psalm 4:8). David had learned to trust in God so completely that he could lie down and sleep even in times of great danger. He had discovered that peace does not depend on our surroundings.

In John 14:1, Jesus comforted His disciples, saying, "Let not your heart be troubled." Jesus knew what they would face in the days ahead. He had told them that if the world hated Him, it would hate them too. Then He reminded them of where He was going and why: "I go and prepare a place for you . . . that where I am, there ye may be also" (John 14:3).

Throughout this farewell, Jesus encouraged them to believe His words and to obey His commandments. He assured them that the Father would send the Holy Ghost to dwell within them. Then Jesus gave them something to which they could cling. In verse 27, He said, "Peace I leave with you, my peace I give unto you: not as the world giveth, give I unto you. Let not your heart be troubled, neither let it be afraid."

The disciples must have been hanging onto every word Christ said. Yes, He was leaving, but His peace would remain with them. He was telling them that no matter what took place in their world—even if it were persecution or death—His peace would be in their hearts. Inside they could be calm, serene, and confident that He was with them.

When our soul has found salvation through Jesus Christ, His peace abides in us. In Philippians 4:7, Paul encourages the saints, "And the peace of God, which passeth all understanding, shall keep your hearts and minds through Christ Jesus." In the previous verse, he tells us to be careful for nothing, that is, not to fret or worry about our circumstances, but to take it to God in prayer. When we do so, we can rest in His peace.

The world cannot understand the peace that Christ gives to His people. This will become more evident as the end of time draws near. 2 Peter 3:14 says, "Wherefore, beloved, seeing that ye look for such things, be diligent that ye may be found of him in peace, without spot, and blameless." When the Lord returns for His own, His peace must be found in us if we want to go with Him.

Jesus strengthened His disciples with these words: "These things I have spoken unto you, that in me ye might have peace. In the world ye shall have tribulation: but be of good cheer; I have overcome the world" (John 16:33). As this world grows darker with sin, we know that we, too, will have tribulation if the Lord tarries. However, Christ has given us His peace. We do not need to fear, but we can rest in His peace, confident that He is in control.

Perfect Peace

My little child lies sleeping;
And unaware is he
Of dangers that are lurking;
He rests so peacefully.

If we were like this infant,
Secure in Christ we'd be;
We'd know He is our Refuge,
And rest contentedly.

When Paul was in the prison,
His soul the Saviour kept.
He knew that God was with him,
So peacefully he slept.

Why do we fret and worry?
Why can we not release
Our cares unto the Saviour
Who offers perfect peace?

Come now, and leave your troubles,
And let your worries cease;
The Prince of Peace is watching,
So rest in perfect peace.

Part
SIX

Looking
Heavenward

Scripture reading: Psalm 119:33–40

The Journey
of Life

*T*he journey of life begins at birth with that first squall. Most of us had loving parents who cuddled us and played with us, teaching us to respect authority and our elders. We were probably taken to church and taught about Jesus at an early age. What must life be like for those who have not had this early nurturing? Maybe they were neglected, abused, or forsaken. Perhaps they never heard the name of Christ except as a curse word spoken in anger.

From birth, a baby recognizes his mother's voice and is attuned to her moods. As the child grows, he begins to emulate his parents. The child reasons that whatever they do must be right, so he follows their example. How easily the tree is bent when it is young, tender, and pliable.

Then the child reaches the stage when he has become a youth with a mind of his own. He doesn't think he needs to listen to his parents anymore. He can decide for himself where he will go, how long he will stay, and what he will do. If the young person has been raised in a God-fearing home, hopefully his mentality will be different. But the time comes when he needs the freedom to make some decisions on his own while still being guided by the loving counsel of his parents. If he has not yet yielded his life to the Lord, it is time for us to pray mightily that he do so. The path that he takes as he leaves his parents' home and authority will be greatly affected by his choice to serve Christ or not. Some people think a young person should go out and sow his wild oats, then settle down and join the church. This fails to take into account the law of sowing and reaping—the cost one will pay for his sins, even if he repents in the future.

The longer one refuses to humble himself before God, the harder it becomes, as the heart becomes hardened to the Spirit's voice. As a person advances into midlife, his love for God may cool. Perhaps the cares of a family, work, pleasures, or lack of time spent in prayer or reading the Word of God may prompt him to neglect spiritual things, pushing them aside with the thought, "I'll do it tomorrow."

When he finally enters the "golden years," it may take an awakening from God to help him see where he is in his spiritual life.

And what about us? We may have been following Jesus for years, but have lost our first love. The maturity we possess at this time of life should make us more zealous for Christ than ever before. Knowing that it won't be long before we leave this life should be an incentive to work harder for the Lord. True, at this time of life, poor health often becomes an issue, yet there is still a work for us to do. Our children and grandchildren and others need our prayers, especially as the world continues to become more estranged from God.

1 Chronicles 29:15 says, "For we are strangers . . . and sojourners, as were all our fathers: our days on the earth are as a shadow, and there is none abiding." Wherever we are in the journey of life, life is short. We need to surrender to Christ and let Him lead us along life's road. He is the Way, the Truth, and the Life (John 14:6). Christ will never abandon His own. He will lead us home.

On a Journey

We are pilgrims on a journey
Marching through this barren land,
Heading for a better country,
Led by God's almighty hand.

God is leading through the darkness,
Like a fire He goes before,
And we feel His love above us,
Guiding cloud from heaven's shore.

Though we're weary, we won't linger,
Like a flint we've set our face;
Homeward bound, our hearts are singing,
"We are kept by Jesus' grace."

There is nothing that can stop us
Till we reach that promised land,
Where we'll see the face of Jesus,
And behold His nail-scarred hands.

We are pilgrims on a journey.
We are pressing onward still,
Longing for that celebration
When we stand on Zion's hill.

Learning to
Drive

As a mother of seven, I've spent quite a bit of time in the front passenger seat coaching a teenager with a new driver's permit. Usually, it wasn't too scary. Most of them seemed to catch on quickly. However, when our fourth child climbed into the driver's seat after getting his permit, I perched on the edge of my seat for the ride home. After reminding my son several times to keep the steering wheel steady, I placed my hand on the wheel. On the way home, I cautioned him about slowing for the railroad tracks, pointed out stop signs, and sometimes exclaimed, "Don't brake so hard!"

When teaching our children to drive, we told them to focus on the road ahead, not on the hood of the car. That helped to drive in a straight line. How true this is in our Christian walk as well. We need to keep our focus on Christ. When we take our eyes off Him, we veer off the straight path.

We reminded our children to watch for railroad crossings, slow or curve signs, stop signs, and traffic lights. We always need to be alert when driving. In our walk with the Lord, there are warnings too. When we sense a red light, do we stop and check for danger? We know that the enemy of our soul will try to get us off track, so we must stay alert. A caution sign should cause us to pray, and proceed slowly. Sometimes we see a sign that says, "DO NOT ENTER." We need to obey this sign, for there is danger ahead if we keep going.

In Proverbs 4:14–15, God warns us: "Enter not into the path of the wicked, and go not in the way of evil men. Avoid it, pass not by it, turn from it, and pass away." We need to heed God's Word and follow His instructions.

Just as I sat near my son when he drove, and sometimes gave him advice or put a hand on the wheel, Jesus offers to guide us if we are willing to listen. We need to ask Him to lead us, and we must follow His road map, the Bible. If we want to get to our destination, we must be vigilant. We don't want to take a wrong turn and end up lost. Proverbs 4:26–27 says, "Ponder the path of thy feet, and let all thy ways be established. Turn not to the right hand, nor to the left: remove thy foot from evil."

Psalm 16, verses 8 and 11, paints a picture of our experience when we allow the Lord to be our guide: "I have set the LORD always before me: because he is at my right hand, I shall not be moved. Thou wilt shew me the path of life: in thy presence is fullness of joy; at thy right hand there are pleasures forevermore."

Let's stay on that straight path that leads to eternal joy. We must not waver in our steadfastness to Christ, but keep our focus on Him. May we say with the Apostle Paul, "I press toward the mark for the prize of the high calling of God in Christ Jesus" (Philippians 3:14). Let's not be deterred by distractions around us, but do as Colossians 3:1–2 admonishes us, "Set your affection on things above, not on things on the earth." When we reach our final destination, it will be worth it all.

Keep My Focus True

Too oft I've let my vision sweep
From heaven to earthly pleasures cheap,

Forgetting they must rust and fade,
Unlike the jewels in heaven laid.

Lord, help me keep my focus true,
And godly things in life pursue;

That when this life is at an end,
To glory land my soul shall wend.

Christl
Is Risen!

In the Gospels, several accounts record how Jesus tried to prepare His disciples for His suffering and death. He foretold His rejection by the Jewish religious leaders, His suffering, and His death. Jesus also told them that on the third day He would rise from the dead.

The disciples did not want to think of this happening to their beloved Master. Although they did not understand His words, they did not ask Him to explain. (See Mark 8:31; 10:32–34.)

As Jesus and His disciples walked to the Mount of Olives where He would be betrayed, Jesus reminded them that after He was risen, He would go before them into Galilee to meet them there. Yet, when their Master was crucified and laid in the tomb, it seemed that in their grief and disappointment, the disciples forgot the promises of His resurrection. How often we are like that! When distressing times are upon us, we forget the very promises to which we should cling.

Even the faithful women who stood near the cross until Jesus died forgot the promise of His resurrection until they were reminded by the angel in the tomb. Not believing the women's story, Peter and John went to the tomb to see for themselves that Christ was not there (John 20:2–8). That evening as the disciples gathered behind closed doors for fear of the Jews, Jesus appeared to them (John 20:19). He showed them His hands, feet, and side. Finally, they believed He was really alive. Thomas, however, who was not present, would not believe their report. He said he must see for himself, and touch the nail prints and Christ's pierced side. Eight days later, Jesus appeared again and told Thomas to touch the nail prints and His side. Thomas cried, "My Lord and my God." Jesus responded, "Blessed are they that have not seen, and yet have believed" (John 20:29).

Believing is essential—believing Jesus is the Son of God, believing He is the Christ who died for us, believing He rose from the grave, and believing that through Christ we have eternal life.

In a day when many say it does not matter what we believe, we must remember the words in 1 John 5:4–5, "For whosoever is born of God overcometh the world: and this is the victory that overcometh the world, even our faith. Who is he that overcometh the world, but he that believeth that Jesus is the Son of God?" Our only hope is in the resurrected Christ.

Jesus promised that He would return again for His bride, the church. Because we believe Christ arose, we have confidence that He conquered sin and the grave, and we have experienced His saving grace through faith in His name. When Christ returns, He will bring with Him the saints who have died. Then those saints who remain alive ". . . shall be caught up . . . to meet the Lord in the air: and so shall we ever be with the Lord" (1 Thessalonians 4:17–18). Hallelujah! Christ is risen, and we believe.

Mary at the Tomb

I came to the tomb in the early dawn,
With tear-washed cheeks, for my Master's gone.
The tomb stood ajar; nothing lay within
Except for the clothes He was buried in.

And then in the tomb, the angels I saw,
Their countenance gleamed; I was filled with awe.
One asked why I wept, told me not to fear.
"I'm looking for Jesus, but He's not here."

I turned to depart with my tear-dimmed eyes,
And glimpsed through the door someone else nearby.
Perhaps he's the gardener; could he help me?
I walked up and tendered my earnest plea.

My tears overflowed as I hid my face.
"Please, sir—tell me true—do you know the place
Where someone has taken and hidden my Lord?"
And then came the voice that my heart adored.

I turned as I heard on His lips my name,
Then looked in His eyes—He was still the same.
I knelt at His feet, while my spirit soared;
For talking to me was my risen Lord!

A Heritage
Forever

My husband and I enjoy genealogies. To help our children appreciate their heritage, I compiled scrapbooks for each of our seven children including pictures, stories, and their family tree. Our lives have been enriched by learning about these things. Usually we think of our heritage as something we acquired when we were born into our family—the traditions or customs we received from our parents and grandparents. We may incorporate them into our family or decide to create new traditions. Some people may feel like there is not much to appreciate about their background. Certainly, as I researched my family tree, I unearthed a few stories of shameful lives.

In Psalm 119:111, the psalmist says, "Thy testimonies have I taken as an heritage for ever: for they are the rejoicing of my heart." Let's listen to what he is saying. He has taken God's testimonies, or promises, as his heritage. He is claiming a right to the promises of God. God is our Father, and He has given us many promises that show His love and care for us, His children. We, too, can claim them as our heritage, which will make our hearts rejoice.

But what if our parents never taught us the ways of God? Or what if we don't even know who our parents are? It's not that important, as long as we realize that God knows us, and He loves us. He invites us to be a part of His family. In God's family, all are equal. God accepts us and adopts us as we come to Him through His Son, Jesus Christ.

No matter what our age or nationality, Jesus calls us to come to Him and, through faith, become His sons and daughters.

Galatians 3:28–29 asserts, "There is neither Jew nor Greek, there is neither bond nor free, there is neither male nor female: for ye are all one in Christ Jesus. And if ye be Christ's, then are ye Abraham's seed, and heirs according to the promise." Galatians 4:7 confirms that we are heirs of God: "Wherefore thou art no more a servant, but a son; and if a son, then an heir of God through Christ." An heir is one who inherits something from someone, usually from a parent. In Psalm 47:4, the psalmist speaks of God choosing an inheritance for us. A cross reference to this verse is 1 Peter 1:3–5. Verse 4 describes our inheritance as "incorruptible and undefiled," which does not fade away, and is laid up in heaven for us. Verse 5 tells us that this inheritance is for those who are kept by the power of God through faith in Jesus Christ. We must claim Jesus as our Redeemer. 1 Peter 1:18–19 reminds us that we were not redeemed by silver or gold, but with the precious blood of Christ.

May we rejoice in our heritage in Christ and live each day to please Him. If we are faithful and obedient unto the end, we will receive the inheritance laid up for us. May we rejoice in God's testimonies as David did, claiming them as our heritage forever.

Adopted

I believed on the Lord and confessed my sin,
Was baptized in His name and was born again.

I've a brand new life; God's adopted me,
Yes, now I'm a part of His family.

No longer a slave, I have kinship rights,
And thus I'll remain if I stay contrite.

Like His firstborn Son, I adore the King;
I'm His child and heir; He's my everything.

I'm excited to follow my Lord each day,
Think upon His Word, bow my knees to pray.

Now I must tell others the happy news,
They can all be heirs; Jesus loves them too!

I'm a child of the King, ransomed by His grace,
And someday I will live in His heavenly place.

The Light

hen I first took up painting, I read many art books. From them I learned the importance of light—its source, its direction, its effect on what it touches, the shadows it casts. All of these must be taken into consideration before starting a painting. Many artists have tried to reproduce the beauty or brilliancy of nature's light, but their work pales in comparison to God's perfect handiwork. Yet artists remain enthralled with light; for some, that focus has had a profound effect on their lives.

Jesus spoke words that may have startled His hearers. In John 8:12, He said, "I am the light of the world: he that followeth me shall not walk in darkness, but shall have the light of life." When the Jews questioned him, Jesus said, "Ye are of this world; I am not of this world" (John 8:23). He further explained that the Father had sent Him into this world and that He does the will of the Father.

From these Scriptures, we understand that Jesus is the Light of the world and that He came from the Father. As the Light, His source and direction was the Father. What effect did Christ's coming and His light have on this world? Not everyone welcomed the light. Jesus said in John 3:20, "Men loved darkness rather than light, because their deeds were evil." They did not want to come to the light, for their deeds would be made known. The light reveals sin. Jesus warned people to walk in the light, lest darkness overcome them, causing them to lose their way. He encouraged them to believe in Him, the Light, that they might be the children of light.

Jesus came to die so that we could live. He saves us and calls us to a holy calling as children of light. Jesus said that as long as He is in this world, He is the Light of the world. He calls us the light of the world (Matthew 5:14–16). We are not to hide the light, but to let it shine so that men will glorify God because of what we do. 1 Peter 2:9 both encourages and challenges us as children of light: "But ye are a chosen generation, a royal priesthood, an holy nation, a peculiar people; that ye should shew forth the praises of him who hath called you out of darkness into his marvelous light." Does Jesus fill us with wonder? Do we rejoice that He called us out of darkness into His light? Do we tell others what He has done for us? Do we praise His name everywhere we go?

Many artists spend a lifetime trying to capture the nuances of light on canvas or film. They wait in cramped, uncomfortable places to catch just the right light. They get up before dawn to see the sun peeking over the horizon and observe its effect until evening. Then they display to the world what they have seen and experienced. How can we do less when we have had an encounter with the Light of lights, the Lord Jesus Christ?

Jesus Is the Light

Based on 1, 2, and 3 John

Jesus is the Light that shone in this world suffused in night,
But so many refused to see, ignoring truth and right.

Jesus came not to condemn, but to save their precious souls,
To offer life in place of death, and broken hearts make whole.

From creation's dawn, Christ knew He must come to earth to die,
Thus with love and compassion, He became sin's sacrifice.

With His own pure, sinless blood, our redemption Jesus bought;
For every tribe and nation was this great salvation wrought.

In the Bible we are told that we must walk in light,
And if we walk in darkness, we are not behaving right.

But a promise God has given—our sins He will forgive;
If we come to Him confessing, then we shall surely live.

We cannot claim to walk in light and hate our brother too;
That's nothing but deception; we must do what's right and true.

We must walk in truth and love as Jesus has commanded us,
For if we are born of God, we will keep His Word; we must!

The
Treasure Chest

For many years, an antique trunk sat in my upstairs. My father had used it as a lad when he went to work for various people for his room and board. Later it held keepsakes from my oldest sister who had died before I was born. Sometimes my mother would allow me to carefully lift out its treasures. I would examine each article: a school bag and its contents, Sunday school papers, a beautiful porcelain doll, a small purse, and a white baptismal dress. These were special items because they had belonged to a beloved person in our family.

I often open another treasure chest—the Word of God. I ponder its contents. Here I can read and study the very words of God. I can hold them close and hide them in my heart. When we dip into the treasure chest of God's Word, we find unsearchable riches. God's promises span the ages, encouraging the saints who have embraced them. In Deuteronomy 31:6, Moses encourages the children of Israel, "Be strong and of a good courage, fear not, nor be afraid of them: for the LORD thy God, he it is that doth go with thee; he will not fail thee, nor forsake thee." Our God is the same today.

Jesus tells us in John 8:36, "If the Son therefore shall make you free, ye shall be free indeed." Christ promises us freedom from sin. John 6:47 assures us if we believe on Christ, we will have everlasting life. In John 16:33, Jesus tells us that we can have peace as we abide in Him. Even though we have tribulations in this world, Jesus says to be of good cheer, for He has overcome the world. Jesus prays for us in John 17:26, that the love with which God loved Him would also be in us, and Christ in us. When we love God, we show it by keeping His commandments. Jesus says in John 14:21 that when we do this we will be loved by the Father, and Christ will love us and will manifest Himself to us.

Our reading for today contains a glorious promise. How wonderful to look forward to the time when Christ returns for His own and we shall forever be with the Lord! Jesus said in John 14:2–3 that in His Father's house are many mansions, and He is going to prepare a place for us: "And if I go and prepare a place for you, I will come again, and receive you unto myself; that where I am, there ye may be also."

God's Word is a treasure chest that never becomes depleted. As we surrender our hearts to Christ, His promises encourage us and strengthen our faith in Him. He is always faithful. His Word is sure. Let's savor the unsearchable riches of God's Word; we will be blessed.

The Word of God

The Word of God is excellent,
We hold it in our hands to read
In our own tongue, God's holy words,
Designed to meet our every need.

How oft do we neglect this gift,
Inspired of God, by prophets penned,
So all could know the way to God?
For all are lost, and all have sinned.

Throughout the ages there have been
The faithful few who chose to stand
For truth and right, and bore the cross
That we may hold His Word in hand.

Absorb the words and hold them dear,
And cherish them with love and care,
Then let them change your very life;
Do not ignore them; do not dare!

Then look around you; see the needs:
So many languish for this Bread.
Their hunger pangs will only cease
When they on living words have fed.

Proclaim it freely; shout the news;
Tell those you know what God can do.
Hold out to them the Bread of Life,
So they can come to know Christ too.

The
Wild Violet

It was springtime, and I was preparing my flowerbed. I had mentioned earlier to the children that I needed to buy some plants. A little later one of my sons called, "Mom, come see what I got for you." Grinning from ear to ear, he presented his gift to me. On his shovel sat a lovely wild violet. My son helped me carefully place it in the flowerbed. He watered and weeded it from time to time. Under our tender care, the violet flourished. The following year there were more violets. Some might look at the wild violets encroaching our flowerbed and wonder, "Why don't you get rid of them?" But when I see them, I remember my son's gift of love, and I cherish their beauty.

Is that how God views us? Colossians 1:21–22 says, "And you, that were sometime alienated and enemies in your mind by wicked works, yet now hath he reconciled in the body of his flesh through death, to present you holy and unblameable and unreproveable in his sight."

Perhaps the Saviour says, "Look, Father, here is one of my own. I brought her out of that wild and dark place. I nurtured her and cared for her. I washed and watered her with my blood and the Word. See how she has grown and flourished. See her beautiful blooms! She has responded so well to my care. She surrendered to my weeding and pruning. She is faultless, Father, perfect in my sight. I present her to you."

Ephesians 5:25–27 tells us that Christ loved the church, and gave Himself for it ". . . that he might present it to himself a glorious church, not having spot, or wrinkle, or any such thing; but that it should be holy and without blemish." Do we surrender ourselves to His pruning, allowing His Spirit to show us the way we should walk? Or do we allow the things of this world to taint our relationship with Christ? Do we excuse sin as shortcomings? Do we seek His cleansing to remove every spot and wrinkle, and to become holy and without blemish?

Paul preached Christ the hope of glory, ". . . warning every man, and teaching every man in all wisdom; that he might present every man perfect in Christ Jesus" (Colossians 1:28). Our own righteousness will never be enough. Only through Christ are we perfected and made acceptable to God.

Jude encourages us to trust in Christ, who "is able to keep you from falling, and to present you faultless before the presence of his glory with exceeding joy" (Jude 24). Those who are faithful to Him are precious in His sight. They bring joy to Him. When Paul wrote to the Philippians, he called them his joy and crown and admonished them to stand fast in the Lord (Philippians 4:1). How much more does Christ rejoice when we, His children and His bride, are faithful and true to Him?

May we give ourselves daily to Christ, allowing Him to perfect us. On the great day when He returns, may we not be a disappointment to Him. Let's be a part of the glorious bride whom Christ presents unto Himself. May we cherish Him who loved us so much so that He died to cleanse us from our sins so we could belong to Him.

Christ's Glorious Church

The church of God still marches on,
Though tested sore is she.
Her banner held aloft declares,
"In Christ is victory!"

While others cast aside the truth,
And are by Satan swayed,
God's faithful church will ever be
In holiness arrayed.

Though fierce the battles she must fight,
God's church will yet prevail.
She will emerge Christ's spotless bride,
For truth will never fail.

From age to age God's children rise,
Embrace the truth, and cast
Their lot with His devoted band,
With courage strong and fast.

Take heart, you weary pilgrims, stand,
And upward lift your eyes,
For soon our everlasting King
Will come through eastern skies.

The bride, prepared for Christ her groom,
Will hear His welcome cry,
And we shall follow risen saints
To meet Him in the sky.

Be watching, waiting, faithfully,
A bride adorned for Him.
Christ's church will rise triumphantly,
His bright and shining gem.

The Completed
Puzzle

When our oldest son Mark was five or six, putting puzzles together was one of our favorite pastimes. Whenever we had some spare time, Mark and I sat at our big dining room table setting puzzle pieces in place. My husband would come over to observe for a while. Finally, shaking his head, he'd walk away.

At first, when we look at the many pieces of a puzzle, it seems a daunting task. We can't see how each one will fit together; but one by one, they are placed into position until the picture is complete. When Mark and I finished a puzzle, we would call the rest of the family to rejoice with us over its completion.

Looking back, I believe that time of puzzle fun taught us to persevere. We learned to not give up on a task just because it looked daunting. In our spiritual lives, we must persevere if we want to receive Christ's reward (Revelation 2:10).

In our walk with God, we can't see the completed picture. Just as Mark and I had to persevere to complete our puzzle, so we need to press on, enduring whatever comes. We know our eternal reward will be worth it all. Matthew 10:22 says, "And ye shall be hated of all men for my name's sake: but he that endureth to the end shall be saved." May we say with the Apostle Paul, "I press toward the mark for the prize of the high calling of God in Christ Jesus" (Philippians 3:14). In 2 Timothy 4:7–8, Paul says, "I have fought a good fight, I have finished my course, I have kept the faith: henceforth there is laid up for me a crown of righteousness, which the Lord, the righteous judge, shall give me at that day: and not me only, but unto all them also that love his appearing."

Let's persevere, press on, and never give up. Someday we will be with Christ, and every trial and weary mile will be over. "But thanks be to God, which giveth us the victory through our Lord Jesus Christ" (1 Corinthians 15:57).

Persevere

When it's hard to keep on going,
And you're tempted to give up,
Don't despair, for Jesus gives us
Ample grace to drink the cup.

He has said that He will help us,
Grant us strength to face the trial,
He has promised He will keep us
Through each long and weary mile.

We can't see the perfect picture,
How each trial is proving us,
How endurance through the testings
Reinforces faith and trust.

Perseverance is our motto;
We must strive to enter in.
For a crown awaits the Christian
Who continues to the end.

Walk
Worthy

*A*n elderly, white-haired man stood to testify of God's grace and goodness. Though I was not a Christian at the time, I could sense the Spirit of God as he spoke. I had observed his life and had seen his faithful walk with God. I tried to avoid him after church because I felt uncomfortable when his blue eyes met mine. I felt like he could look right through me and see the sin in my heart. When I became a Christian, however, it was joy to visit with this man and his wife. They encouraged me greatly as a young Christian. Finally, I could meet his eyes without wavering, for I knew I had nothing to hide.

All who believe on Christ are called to walk worthy of Him. This means leaving the old life behind and putting on the new man (Ephesians 4:22, 24). It means living a life dedicated to Jesus Christ. When we call ourselves Christians, the unconverted take notice. They watch to see if our actions match our words. They expect us to have a higher standard than the world does. They are quick to spot a hypocrite. Our testimony is effective only when our actions match our words.

Ephesians 5:8 tells us, "For ye were sometimes darkness, but now are ye light in the Lord: walk as children of light." Ephesians 5:15 says, "See then that ye walk circumspectly, not as fools, but as wise." From the dictionary, I learned that walking *circumspectly* means to "consider the consequences before we act."[19] If our lives fail to portray Christ, we may cause some to turn away from Christ or become discouraged from ever coming to Him.

One of my school classmates once remarked that he wished he could stand for the Lord, too, but he wanted to fit in with others. Their acceptance of him was more important to him than obedience to Christ.

My husband was a young Christian when he attended the local fair. An acquaintance saw him there, and told him, "I didn't think I would see you here. I thought you were a Christian." That comment made him reconsider the choice he had made. That was the last fair he attended. We never know who is watching us, but we can be sure that someone is. May we never be guilty of leading others down the wrong path.

Christ wants a glorious church without spot or wrinkle, holy, and without blemish (Ephesians 5:27). Even as a bride wants to please her bridegroom, so we should strive to please Christ. Does our walk bring glory and honor to Him? Do those who observe us see that we belong to Christ? We have a high calling as the children of God. May we walk worthy of our vocation.

Walk in Truth

Walk in the truth, and you will find
Light to guide and peace of mind,

As the Father's strengthening grace
Guides you through life's darkest place.

Seek to live as Jesus taught;
Love each other as you ought;

Keep His Word throughout the day;
Follow on the narrow way.

Then when you stand on Judgment Day,
You will hear your Jesus say,

"Enter, true and faithful one;
The race is o'er, the victory won."

Weighed in
the Balances

*I*n today's reading, Belshazzar, king of the Chaldeans, held a feast for a thousand of his lords. As he tasted the wine, he remembered the golden vessels which his father had taken from the temple in Jerusalem. He called for them to be brought out so he and his guests could drink wine from them. They drank from the sacred vessels, even as they praised the gods of gold, silver, brass, iron, wood, and stone.

While Belshazzar was reveling with his lords, the fingers of a man's hand appeared, writing on the wall. As the king saw it, his merriment ceased, his thoughts became troubled, and his knees began to shake. He wondered what this could mean. Immediately, King Belshazzar called for his wise men and astrologers, but they could not help him. Then the queen suggested he call for Daniel the Hebrew to interpret the writing.

When Daniel appeared, he spoke first to the king about his father, Nebuchadnezzar, to whom God had given a kingdom, majesty, honor, and glory. However, when his heart was lifted up and his mind hardened in pride, he had been deposed from his kingdom, stripped of his glory. For seven years he had lived like a beast, eating grass. His hair grew long like feathers, and his nails like birds' claws. At the end of that time, his sanity returned and his kingdom was restored. He said, "Now I Nebuchadnezzar praise and extol and honour the King of heaven, all whose works are truth, and his ways judgment: and those that walk in pride he is able to abase" (Daniel 4:37).

Daniel continued, "And thou his son, O Belshazzar, hast not humbled thine heart, though thou knewest all this" (Daniel 5:22). The king had not only defiled the Lord's vessels, but he had also blasphemed God by praising false gods instead of giving honor and praise to the one true God.

Then Daniel gave Belshazzar the interpretation of the handwriting: God has numbered your kingdom, and finished it. You are weighed in the balances, and found wanting. Your kingdom is divided and given to the Medes and Persians.

That very night King Belshazzar was slain, and Darius the Median took over his kingdom. Belshazzar's pride was his downfall. He had not learned from his father's humiliation.

In today's world when we hear leaders applauding themselves, bragging about what they will do, we do well to remember that God still appoints rulers over kingdoms. He is able to depose as well. May we take heed to ourselves and not allow pride in our lives in any form. We must always give God glory for whatever our feeble hands and minds may do. We are helpless to accomplish anything without God. Our every breath is a gift from Him. May we live for God's glory and honor alone.

In the Balance Weighed

There is a soul in the balance weighed—
What will the judgment be today?
Has the blood of Jesus been applied?
If not, this soul shall surely die.

There is a soul in the balance weighed—
What will the Saviour have to say?
Eternal life was offered you.
Have you obeyed, to Christ been true?

There is a soul in the balance weighed—
To be received, or cast away.
Are the things of earth worth what you'll pay
When you face God on Judgment Day?

There is a soul in the balance weighed—
Does Christ live in your heart today?
Don't be denied on Judgment Day;
Come to the Lord without delay.

And the World
Passeth Away

ecently I heard someone say that at one time people predicted that by now our world would be unable to grow anything. The speaker remarked that since that time, our corn production alone has doubled. This reminded me of God's promise in Genesis 8:22: "While the earth remaineth, seedtime and harvest, and cold and heat, and summer and winter, and day and night shall not cease." God made this promise when Noah offered a burnt offering after the flood. God also promised to never again flood the entire earth. As a sign of this covenant, God set His rainbow in the sky.

We cannot trust the predictions of men. If they do not align with the Word of God, they will not come to pass. Sometimes people become so concerned about this earthly planet that they focus all their energy on preserving it. Although we shouldn't be careless with the earth or its resources, we should be more concerned about our responsibility to God and to our fellow man.

God is the One who made the world in the first place. He alone determines how long it will stand; our puny efforts to improve the atmosphere, to "go green," to cultivate environmentally friendly practices will not alter the fact that the timeline of this world is in God's hands. Hebrews 1:10–12 puts this in perspective for us: "And, Thou, Lord, in the beginning hast laid the foundation of the earth; and the heavens are the work of thine hands: they shall perish; but thou remainest; and they all shall wax old as doth a garment; and as a vesture shalt thou fold them up, and they shall be changed: but thou art the same, and thy years shall not fail."

2 Peter 3:10 reminds us that this world will not last forever: "The heavens shall pass away with a great noise, and the elements shall melt with fervent heat, the earth also . . . shall be burned up." The next verse tells us how we ought to live now, in light of the fact that someday these things will take place. We will be prepared to face these cataclysmic events if we are living godly, holy lives. As Christians, we have a hope in that day. We will see a new heaven and a new earth if we are found blameless and at peace with God.

Merely calling ourselves Christians is no safety net. God sees our hearts. He knows if we are masquerading as something we are not. He knows our carelessness regarding His Word, our shallowness toward Him. If Christ returned today and all these things came to pass, would we be ready?

1 John 2:6 tells us that if we say we abide in Christ, we should also walk as He walked. Verse 15 admonishes us further: "Love not the world, neither the things that are in the world. If any man love the world, the love of the Father is not in him." Verse 17 reminds us that everything we see is temporal: "And the world passeth away, and the lust thereof: but he that doeth the will of God abideth for ever."

We cannot save planet earth. We cannot even save ourselves. Only by God's grace, through faith in Jesus Christ and His blood, can we become children of God. We need not fear the end of the world, but rather, we should rejoice in the coming of our Saviour and Redeemer. Only in Christ is true safety. Let's believe on Him today, and be steadfast unto the end.

Found Wanting?

When your life is over someday,
You must give account of your deeds;
What if your name's not in the Book?
Will you like what God has to say?

If you've heaped up treasures to store,
Neglected the needy and poor,
Will you hang your head there in shame
When you're turned away at the door?

If on human strength you've relied
To live a life holy and good,
It won't be enough on that day
If the blood of the Lamb's not applied.

If your name's on the membership roll
Of a prominent church in the town,
But sin has control of your life,
You will find no hope for your soul.

Should the Lord say you must depart,
Depart, for you're not of His fold,
You'll wish you had humbled yourself,
And let Jesus into your heart.

Will you be found wanting that day?
Will Christ turn and send you away?
When He sits upon His white throne,
Tell me, what will He have to say?

Friend, the Saviour is calling today;
Believe, and repent, and be saved,
For Jesus alone is the Way
To be ready for Judgment Day.

But a Step

When David told his friend Jonathan, King Saul's son, about Saul's plan to kill David, Jonathan protested. He was unaware of this threat. David, however, assured Jonathan, "There is but a step between me and death" (1 Samuel 20:3). One moment we have life, and in just a step, our life can be snuffed out. Death takes many forms—accidents, disease, or old age. Sometimes we know beforehand that death is imminent. Other times it is swift and unexpected.

In Ezekiel 18:4, God pronounces judgment: "The soul that sinneth, it shall die." In light of this truth, He encourages the children of Israel to repent and change their ways so they will live and not die. In verse 32, He says, "For I have no pleasure in the death of him that dieth . . . wherefore turn yourselves, and live ye."

What a contrast there is between the death of the wicked and the death of a saint. Psalm 116:15 tells us, "Precious in the sight of the LORD is the death of his saints." God is grieved when people die in their sins, but the death of the righteous is a precious, wonderful thing, for it ushers them into His presence.

The finality of death causes many to fear it. The Apostle Paul wrote to the church at Philippi expressing his desire to magnify Christ whether by life or by death: "For to me to live is Christ, and to die is gain" (Philippians 1:21). Paul did not fear death. He knew there would be joy when he took that last step, for he would be with his Lord forever.

The ultimate example of how to face death is portrayed in Jesus. Although He pled with His Father that He might not drink the cup of death, He accepted the Father's will, facing the cross with courage in obedience to His Father (Matthew 26:39). Philippians 2:9 underscores this by saying that Christ humbled Himself and became obedient unto death, even the death of the cross. 2 Timothy 1:10 speaks of ". . . Jesus Christ, who hath abolished death, and hath brought life and immortality to light through the gospel." Jesus promised that all who believe on Him should have everlasting life. They won't be condemned, but will pass "from death unto life" (John 5:24).

Hebrews 2:9 tells us how Christ came to "taste death for every man." Verses 14–15 say Christ became flesh and blood, suffering death "that through death he might destroy him that had the power of death, that is, the devil; and deliver them who through fear of death were all their lifetime subject to bondage."

If we believe in Christ and the work He has done for us, we do not need to fear death. Christ has won the victory! It is through faith in His name that we can fearlessly take that final step out of this world. Hebrews 3:14 motivates us to endure: "For we are made partakers of Christ, if we hold the beginning of our confidence steadfast unto the end." Jesus said in Revelation 2:10, "Be thou faithful unto death, and I will give thee a crown of life."

There is but a step between us and death. With our confidence in Christ, we can step joyfully through that door, anticipating what lies beyond.

My Soul Shall Soar

I shall forever sing Christ's praise,
For from the dead my soul He raised
To walk no more in paths of sin,
For through His name I'm born again.

And when my body yields to death,
And draws one final, fleeting breath,
My living soul shall soar above
To live in pure delight and love.

The grave cannot the victory win
For one who's been released from sin;
This body shall be raised anew
When Christ returns for all the true.

The Brevity
of Life

When elderly people talk about their lives, one of the things they often say is that life is short. How true this is! My husband and I have been married fifty-some years now. How quickly those years have sped. As Job said, "My days are swifter than a weaver's shuttle" (Job 7:6).

Our lives are filled with making a living, caring for our families, pursuing hobbies, going to church, visiting, vacationing, and engaging in other interests. Each day gets filled to the brim, leaving us unable to accomplish all we intended to do.

James 4:14 says, "For what is your life? It is even a vapour, that appeareth for a little time, and then vanisheth away." Frequently we hear of someone whose life has ended. The person may be young or old, your age, or mine. Death is no respecter of persons. Often death comes without warning. Solomon wrote about this in Ecclesiastes 9:12: "For man also knoweth not his time: as the fishes that are taken in an evil net, and as the birds that are caught in the snare; so are the sons of men snared in an evil time, when it falleth suddenly upon them."

The psalmist compares the length of a person's life to a shadow: "My days are like a shadow that declineth; and I am withered like grass. But thou, O LORD, shalt endure for ever; and thy remembrance unto all generations" (Psalm 102:11–12). Like the evening shadows that grow shorter and shorter until they are swallowed up in the darkness of night, so is our life. Our days on earth pass quickly, speeding toward the time of our departure.

1 Peter 1:23–25 speaks of us who have been born again, "not of corruptible seed, but of incorruptible, by the word of God, which liveth and abideth for ever." Even though our outward man, our body, will die and decay, our souls will live forever with Christ. Verse 24 says, "For all flesh is as grass, and all the glory of man as the flower of grass. The grass withereth, and the flower thereof falleth away." All flesh is as grass. We cannot trust the arm of flesh to save us. We are all helpless to save ourselves or others. Our only Saviour is Christ, the Word of God.

Since our life is but a vapor, we need to pray as the psalmist did in Psalm 90:12, "So teach us to number our days, that we may apply our hearts unto wisdom." Jesus said, "Where your treasure is, there will your heart be also" (Matthew 6:21). Are we seeking to store up treasures here, or in heaven? Our earthly wealth will perish, but what is done for Christ will last, for it is laid up in heaven.

Even if we live to be a hundred years old or more, compared to eternity, our life is but a moment. As we heed the Word of God and consider the brevity of life and the certainty of His Word, may we live to glorify God, working for His kingdom. While we have life and breath, let's praise our Maker and Redeemer. "He will be our guide even unto death" (Psalm 48:14).

Teach Us to Number Our Days

Like the flowers that blossom, but too quickly fade,
Our lives are soon over, and we go to the grave.

Like the grass, once so vibrant, is cut down and dies,
So our days soon are ended, and our soul homeward flies.

As the mist that we see, which so soon disappears,
The vapor of life fades away with the years;

When our days here shall end like a tale that is told,
Will our soul take its flight up to glories untold?

For our flesh is as grass, and its glory shall fade
Like the petals of flowers that soon fall away;

Yet the Word of our God will forever endure.
Put your faith in the Lord; make your destiny sure.

So then teach us, O Father, to number our days,
And help us to walk in your precepts today;

Father, quicken our hearts, so when life here is done,
Our spirits shall fly, to live on with your Son.

Go Ye into
All the World

Two of my husband's classmates felt called to go to Africa after their training was finished. One of the young men often talked about what he would do when he got to Africa. David, the other student, quietly went about organizing a Sunday afternoon Bible class for the neighborhood children. Soon they had outgrown the room they were using, and a larger building was found to rent. If no donations for the work came in, David paid the rent from his own pocket.

When David and his wife took a walk, we would often see several children tagging along. The children loved David and his wife because they loved the children. David did not wait to do the Lord's work until he got to Africa. He saw a mission field right where he was. Someone once said that if we aren't good missionaries at home, we won't be good missionaries on the field.

In Mark 16:15, Jesus commanded His disciples: "Go ye into all the world, and preach the gospel to every creature." In Acts 1:8, He said, "But ye shall receive power, after that the Holy Ghost is come upon you: and ye shall be witnesses unto me both in Jerusalem, and in all Judea, and in Samaria, and unto the uttermost part of the earth." Today the task of reaching the uttermost part of the earth is becoming easier. With air travel, we can be at a distant place in a few hours. Also, innovations like the Internet and the printed Word help to speed the spread of the Gospel.

Our mission field may be as small as our family, our workplace, our school, or as big as our neighborhood. Or perhaps God is calling us to leave home and family to serve Him in another country. One thing we know for sure is that Christ calls all of us to serve Him, to share the Good News with others. When Jesus spoke with the woman at the well, telling her all she had ever done and offering her living water, she could not keep this to herself. She ran into the town, telling them to come see the Christ for themselves (John 4).

When Jesus appointed seventy disciples and sent them out two by two to the cities where He would later go to preach, He said, "The harvest truly is great, but the labourers are few: pray ye therefore the Lord of the harvest, that he would send forth labourers into his harvest" (Luke 10:2). This command is still urgent today.

Jesus appeared to His disciples after His resurrection and said, "Thus it is written, and thus it behoved Christ to suffer, and to rise from the dead the third day: and that repentance and remission of sins should be preached in his name among all nations, beginning at Jerusalem. And ye are witnesses of these things" (Luke 24:46–48).

One day work will cease and time will be no more. All that we would do for Christ must be done now. Jesus said, "The night cometh, when no man can work" (John 9:4). While Jesus was here, He was the Light of the world. Now we are called to be lights in this dark world, pointing others to Christ, the Light. May we be about our Father's business, sharing the Gospel of Jesus Christ—in all the world.

Have I Cared Enough?

As I tend my business, I'm amazed what I see
In the throngs of humanity passing by me.

There are some plodding on, by their life beaten down;
And there're some so unhappy, they can't seem but to frown.

I see those who press forward in a mad, restless urge,
So intent on their destiny, like waves they surge.

In the depths of their conscience, do they know their great need?
If I tried to address them, would my words make them heed?

If I told them of Jesus and the way He forgives,
Would they slow down to listen to the hope that He gives?

I won't know of the outcome of my words lest I dare
To reach out in compassion, show that I really care.

Times to speak about Jesus quickly hurry on by,
For our days upon earth are like vapors that fly.

Have I done what was needed, never sparing the cost,
To reach out to the hurting and to rescue the lost?

Anticipating

*I*t was 1964, and I was a senior in high school looking forward to graduation. My plans for graduation, however, paled in significance beside those for my wedding. Just eleven days after the special ceremony marking the completion of twelve years of school, I would take part in another ceremony, this time to become the bride of my beloved. How eagerly I anticipated that day!

The dictionary gives these three meanings of the verb *anticipate:* "(1) Act beforehand to address something imminent: to imagine or consider something before it happens, and make any necessary preparations. (2) Expect something: to think or be fairly sure that a certain thing will happen or come. (3) Look forward to something: to feel excited, hopeful, or eager about something that is going to happen."[20]

I remember all the preparations I had made for my wedding day. My dress was purchased, the attendants' dresses made, the service planned, the caterer consulted for the reception, the minister asked to perform the vows, and the guests invited. Everything was ready. The groom had promised to be there. I did not expect anything to go wrong because I had done all I could to insure that things would go smoothly.

The wedding was to take place at our church at two o'clock in the afternoon on May 30. I felt very excited, hopeful, and eager as I waited for that special day to come. As Christians, we, too, should eagerly anticipate an event that will certainly happen—the return of our Lord Jesus Christ. Shortly before His death, Jesus gave His disciples a promise. In John 14, Jesus was trying to prepare them for His death and ascension to the Father. He said in verse 3, "And if I go and prepare a place for you, I will come again, and receive you unto myself; that where I am, there ye may be also."

Just as I prepared for my wedding, we should be preparing for Christ's return. Like the disciples, we must believe that Jesus is the Son of God who died on the cross, shed His blood, and became the perfect sacrifice for our sins. We must believe Jesus rose again and is at the Father's right hand, making intercession to the Father for us. We must ask Christ to forgive our sins, and we must turn from our old life to walk in newness of life.

In 2 Peter 3, Peter reminds us of the Lord's return. Verse 12 tells us that we should be looking for and hasting, or greatly desiring, the day of Christ's return. We, the church, are Christ's bride. If we are prepared as a bride for her wedding, we will eagerly anticipate that day.

Verses 11 and 14 tell us how we need to live to be ready for Christ's return. We must be holy and godly, at peace with God, and without spot or wrinkle. 1 John 2:28 encourages us, "And now, little children, abide in him; that when he shall appear, we may have confidence, and not be ashamed before him at his coming." May we be ready to meet the Lord with the light of anticipation on our faces.

In the Twinkling of an Eye

Someday soon we'll see Christ coming
Through the clouds in bright array.
With a shout and trumpet sounding,
He will call His bride away.

All the dead in Christ shall rise up;
In the air we all shall be.
Christ will change these earthly bodies,
Give us immortality.

When our Lord comes back to claim us
In the twinkling of an eye,
Will you be among that number
Who will meet Him in the sky?

Are you ready for His coming?
Have you washed in Calvary's flow?
Are you longing for the moment
When He'll call, "It's time to go!"

O be ready, for He's coming
Through the clouds in eastern sky;
Be prepared for that great moment;
Our redemption draweth nigh.

Endnotes

[1] "Fellowship." *Reader's Digest Oxford Complete Wordfinder.* Sarah Tulloch. The Reader's Digest Association, Pleasantville, N. Y., 1993, p. 534.

[2] "Fervent." *Encarta World English Dictionary.* Anne H. Soukhanov. St. Martin's Press, New York, 1999, p. 657.

[3] Adam Clarke, "Proverbs 10:3." Adam Clarke's Commentary on the Bible, Vol. 3: Job to Solomon's Song. Abingdon Press, New York and Nashville, 1967.

[4] "Holy." *Reader's Digest Oxford Complete Wordfinder.* Sarah Tulloch. The Reader's Digest Association, Pleasantville, N. Y., 1993, p. 700.

[5] "Sacrifice." *Encarta World English Dictionary.* Anne H. Soukhanov. St. Martin's Press, New York, 1999, p. 1576.

[6] "Hypocrite." Ibid., p. 887.

[7] "Capability." Ibid., p. 266.

[8] "Meek." Ibid., p. 1124.

[9] "Quiet." Ibid., p. 1473.

[10] Matthew Henry, Commentary of the Whole Bible. Zondervan Publishing, Grand Rapids, 1961, p. 1889.

[11] "Slander." *Reader's Digest Oxford Complete Wordfinder.* Sarah Tulloch. The Reader's Digest Association, Pleasantville, N. Y., 1993, p. 1424.

[12] "Receive." Ibid., p. 1252. The Amplified New Testament. Zondervan Publishing House, Grand Rapids, 1958, p. 594.

[13] "Reverence." *Reader's Digest Oxford Complete Wordfinder.* Sarah Tulloch. The Reader's Digest Association, Pleasantville, N. Y., 1993, p. 1292.

[14] "Test." *Encarta World English Dictionary.* Anne H. Soukhanov. St. Martin's Press, New York, 1999, p. 1842.

[15] "Trial." Ibid., p. 1899.

[16] "Tribulation." Ibid., p. 1900.

[17] "Dismay." Ibid., p. 517.

[18] "Contend." Ibid., p. 392.

[19] "Circumspect." Ibid., p. 332.

[20] "Anticipate." Ibid., p. 72.

About the Author

Wilma Webb lives with her husband of over fifty years near Spencerville, Indiana. They have seven children, twenty-six grandchildren, and one great-grandchild. Wilma enjoys writing not only devotionals and poetry but also songs. After her children were grown, she took up painting in her spare time. Wilma is a member of Hicksville Christian Fellowship in northwest Ohio. She enjoys hearing from readers. You may email her at wilmawebb46@live.com or write to her in care of Christian Aid Ministries, P.O. Box 360, Berlin, OH 44610.

Christian Aid Ministries

Christian Aid Ministries was founded in 1981 as a nonprofit, tax-exempt 501(c)(3) organization. Its primary purpose is to provide a trustworthy and efficient channel for Amish, Mennonite, and other conservative Anabaptist groups and individuals to minister to physical and spiritual needs around the world. This is in response to the command ". . . do good unto all men, especially unto them who are of the household of faith" (Galatians 6:10).

Each year, CAM supporters provide approximately 15 million pounds of food, clothing, medicines, seeds, Bibles, Bible story books, and other Christian literature for needy people. Most of the aid goes to orphans and Christian families. Supporters' funds also help clean up and rebuild for natural disaster victims, put up Gospel billboards in the U.S., support several church-planting efforts, operate two medical clinics, and provide resources for needy families to make their own living. CAM's main purposes for providing aid are to help and encourage God's people and bring the Gospel to a lost and dying world.

CAM has staff, warehouse, and distribution networks in Romania, Moldova, Ukraine, Haiti, Nicaragua, Liberia, and Israel. Aside from management, supervisory personnel, and bookkeeping operations, volunteers do most of the work at CAM locations. Each year, volunteers at our warehouses, field bases, DRS projects, and other locations donate over 200,000 hours of work.

CAM's ultimate purpose is to glorify God and help enlarge His kingdom. ". . . whatsoever ye do, do all to the glory of God" (1 Corinthians 10:31).

The Way to God and Peace

We live in a world contaminated by sin. Sin is anything that goes against God's holy standards. When we do not follow the guidelines that God our Creator gave us, we are guilty of sin. Sin separates us from God, the source of life.

Since the time when the first man and woman, Adam and Eve, sinned in the Garden of Eden, sin has been universal. The Bible says that we all have "sinned and come short of the glory of God" (Romans 3:23). It also says that the natural consequence for that sin is eternal death, or punishment in an eternal hell: "Then when lust hath conceived, it bringeth forth sin: and sin, when it is finished, bringeth forth death" (James 1:15).

But we do not have to suffer eternal death in hell. God provided forgiveness for our sins through the death of His only Son, Jesus Christ. Because Jesus was perfect and without sin, He could die in our place. "For God so loved the world that he gave his only begotten Son, that whosoever believeth in him should not perish, but have everlasting life" (John 3:16).

A sacrifice is something given to benefit someone else. It costs the giver greatly. Jesus was God's sacrifice. Jesus' death takes away the penalty of sin for everyone who accepts this sacrifice and truly repents of their sins. To repent of sins means to be truly sorry for and turn away from the things we have done that have violated God's standards (Acts 2:38; 3:19).

Jesus died, but He did not remain dead. After three days, God's Spirit miraculously raised Him to life again. God's Spirit does something similar in us. When we receive Jesus as our sacrifice and repent of our sins, our hearts are changed. We become spiritually alive! We develop new desires and attitudes (2 Corinthians 5:17). We begin to make choices that please God (1 John 3:9). If we do fail and commit sins, we can ask God for forgiveness. "If we confess our sins, he is faithful and just to forgive us our sins, and to cleanse us from all unrighteousness" (1 John 1:9).

Once our hearts have been changed, we want to continue growing spiritually. We will be happy to let Jesus be the Master of our lives and will want to become more like Him. To do this, we must meditate on God's Word and commune with God in prayer. We will testify to others of this change by being baptized and sharing the good news of God's victory over sin and death. Fellowship with a faithful group of believers will strengthen our walk with God (1 John 1:7).